ANXIOUS ATTACHMENT RECOVERY

PROVEN STEPS TO CONQUER RELATIONSHIP ANXIETY, REBUILD TRUST, AND CULTIVATE LASTING LOVE

ELIZA BENNETT

CONTENTS

INTRODUCTION

I will never forget one night I was sitting alone at home, staring at my phone, my anxiety and panic increasing with each minute that passed without a text. I had a sinking feeling in my stomach. I was convinced that my partner's silence had a secret meaning—that they were pulling away, losing interest, or worse. I knew it was not rational, but the fear gripped me, making it hard to breathe or think clearly. It was a moment of intense relationship anxiety, a feeling many of us know all too well.

Moments like these and my recovery journey led me to write this book. My name is Eliza Bennett, and I have walked the path of overcoming relationship anxiety. I have not only delved into academic research in psychology and attachment theory, but I have also grappled with personal struggles with anxious attachment. I have felt the same fears and struggled with similar insecurities that you may have. This shared experience drives me to provide you with the tools and insights you need to transform your anxious attachment style.

With this experience, I have committed to providing the tools and insights you need to transform your anxious attachment style. Over the years, I have met countless people who have worked through understanding and conquering the difficulties of anxious attachment to have more secure and fulfilling relationships.

WHO THIS BOOKS IS FOR

This book is for anyone who has ever felt anxiety in their relationships. If you often find yourself overthinking messages, worrying about your partner's feelings, or second-guessing your worth, know that you are not alone. This guide is specially crafted for those of us who experience anxious attachment, whether you are in a long-term relationship, dating, or navigating the complexities of love and connection. If you find it hard to trust others or feel insecure about your partner's commitment, this book will provide the insights and strategies you need to navigate these turbulent emotions with confidence.

It is also for those seeking to deepen their knowledge of attachment styles and how they affect their relationships. Whether you are a seasoned psychology reader or new to these concepts, I have used approachable language and well-researched content that will resonate with you. My book aims to empower those who wish to break free from the patterns of anxiety and insecurity that have held them back, offering a roadmap to healthier, more fulfilling connections.

Furthermore, this book will be valuable if you value personal growth and self-awareness. It encourages introspection and offers tools to heal emotional wounds and nurture a sense of inner security. By addressing the roots of anxious attachment, you will embark on a journey toward improving your relationship and overall well-being. Ultimately, this book is for anyone ready to embrace change and take proactive steps toward secure, loving relationships filled with trust and fulfillment.

WHAT TO EXPECT FROM THIS BOOK

In these pages, you will comprehensively understand anxious attachment, its roots, and its impact on your relationships and self-esteem. More importantly, you will discover practical steps to break free from the cycle of anxiety and insecurity. These valuable strategies are theoretical concepts and tools you can apply daily to develop healthier, more secure connections. I wrote this book to equip you with the knowledge and skills to overcome anxious attachment.

This book is structured to take you on a step-by-step journey to understanding and overcoming anxious attachment. Each chapter explores different aspects of this journey, providing actionable steps to implement the strategies daily.

I will first provide a comprehensive overview of anxious attachment, exploring its psychological and neuroscientific underpinnings. You will discover how to identify the specific signs and behaviors linked to this attachment style, both in yourself and others.

After that, I will give you practical strategies and approaches for managing overthinking, anxiety, and jealousy in relationships.

Then, we will explore connecting with and healing our inner child.

We will discuss rebuilding and strengthening our emotional security and trust in our relationships. I will also provide techniques for improving long-term emotional regulation and balance.

I will also guide you in strengthening relationships, including setting the proper boundaries essential to any secure attachment and healthy relationship. The other key topics I will cover in this book include enhancing self-awareness and fostering ongoing personal growth.

HOW TO USE THIS BOOK

To effectively use this book, start by setting aside dedicated time for reading and reflection. Create a quiet, comfortable space to fully engage with the material without distractions. As you read, note key concepts that resonate with you and reflect on your experiences and emotions related to the topics discussed. This process will help you internalize and apply the lessons to your life.

Additionally, consider approaching each chapter with an open mind and a willingness to learn. Some sections may challenge your beliefs or require you to confront difficult emotions. Allow yourself to process these feelings and recognize that discomfort is often a part of growth. After completing a chapter, take the time to journal about your thoughts and any insights you gained. This practice will deepen your understanding and reinforce the ideas presented.

Finally, do not hesitate to revisit certain book sections as needed. Healing and personal growth are non-linear journeys, and different passages resonate with you at various stages of your process. Repeatedly engaging with the material can provide new perspectives and reinforce your commitment to cultivating secure attachments and healthier relationships. Remember, this book is a tool to support you on your path, so use it in a way that feels empowering and nurturing.

EMBRACING THE JOURNEY OF RECOVERY

Anxious attachment is more than just a label—it is a deeply ingrained pattern that shapes how we connect with others, often leaving us feeling vulnerable, insecure, and longing for reassurance in our relationships. Rooted in early experiences and carried into adulthood, this attachment style can create cycles of fear, doubt, and emotional turmoil that impact our romantic partnerships and sense of self-worth. Yet, the fact that anxious attachment stems from learned behaviors means you can unlearn it. I will guide you to understanding these patterns, breaking free from them, and cultivating healthier, more secure relationships. Whether you have struggled with relationship anxiety, experienced recurring trust issues, or felt trapped in a loop of emotional uncertainty, this journey is about reclaiming your emotional balance, rebuilding trust, and creating lasting love—not just with others but also with yourself.

If you are reading this, you are probably looking for comfort, answers, and ways to break free from the cycle of anxiety that has imprisoned you. It is important to remember that you are never alone. Yes, there are many challenges on this journey of healing and personal growth, but the rewards can transform your life. I encourage you to commit to this journey with an open heart and mind. The path to recovery and secure attachment is within your reach. Embrace the process, take each step with intention, and know you can achieve secure connections and lasting love. The adventure toward a more fulfilling and secure relationship starts now.

CHAPTER 1
UNDERSTANDING ANXIOUS ATTACHMENT

ONE EVENING, AFTER A MINOR DISAGREEMENT WITH MY PARTNER, I found myself in a downward spiral of anxiety and worry. I replayed our conversation over and over again, scrutinizing every word. I tormented myself with the idea that this minor conflict signaled the end of our relationship. I could not sleep, my mind racing with thoughts of abandonment and rejection. I experienced raw anxiety, a feeling that many of us with anxious attachment know all too well.

In this chapter, we will explore what anxious attachment is and the roots of feelings like these, giving you insights into why we experience them and how they affect our relationships.

WHAT IS ANXIOUS ATTACHMENT?

Anxious attachment is a term rooted in psychology and neuroscience. It describes a pattern that includes a deep fear of abandonment, as well as an overwhelming need for closeness and reassurance. Negative experiences in childhood are what usually lead us to this attachment style, and it is shaped by our interactions with caregivers. If we have inconsistent or unpredictable bonds with our caregivers when we are children, the seeds of anxious attachment are sown. This can lead to behaviors that tend to disrupt our relationships in adulthood.

Some of the most common signs of being anxiously attached are frequent worrying about what your partner feels and does, constantly seeking validation, and feeling insecure even when there are no apparent issues in the relationship. People with anxious attachments might overthink every conversation, feel intensely jealous for no reason, and look for constant reassurance that they are loved and valued.

Research shows that those with anxious attachment are more likely to experience relationship dissatisfaction, emotional turmoil, and lower self-esteem. Further studies show that nearly 20% of adults exhibit anxious attachment behaviors. If you are among them, you will have enormous difficulty forming stable and fulfilling connections. If you have an anxious attachment style, you will have to do significant work addressing and managing your emotions and the roots of the problem if you want to build healthier, more secure relationships.

THE ROOTS OF ANXIOUS ATTACHMENT

The tendency for humans to develop anxious attachment styles is deeply rooted in our evolutionary past. In early human societies, survival depended on close-knit relationships, and caregiver availability was crucial for the survival of infants. Infants who maintained proximity to a caregiver were more likely to survive, as caregivers provided protection, nourishment, and learning opportunities. This need for closeness and security became hardwired into our brains, ensuring that infants would signal distress when separated, thereby ensuring their caregivers' return.

From an evolutionary perspective, attachment behaviors such as clinging to caregivers and showing distress during separation were advantageous. Infants who exhibited these behaviors were more likely to receive the attention and care they needed, ultimately increasing their chances of survival. Over generations, these behaviors became a fundamental part of human development, shaping how we bond and form relationships.

John Bowlby, a pioneer in attachment theory, underscored the evolutionary perspective. His research revealed that early attachment behaviors served a purpose beyond immediate survival: they helped form a secure base from which a child could explore the world and develop confidence. Bowlby's work laid the foundation for understanding how attachment styles form and persist throughout life, enlightening us about the profound impact of early experiences on our development.

Mary Ainsworth, a colleague of Bowlby, further advanced the field with her pioneering research. Her famous Strange Situation experiment identified three primary attachment styles:

- Secure
- Avoidant
- Anxious

This structured observational study subjected infants to separations and reunions with their caregivers. Securely attached infants showed distress when separated but quickly calmed upon reunion. In contrast, anxiously attached infants exhibited intense distress during separation and had difficulty calming down even when the caregiver returned. Ainsworth's work underscored the variability in attachment behaviors, providing a framework for understanding anxious attachment. We owe much to Ainsworth's pioneering research, which has advanced our understanding of attachment styles.

HOW CHILDHOOD EXPERIENCES SHAPE ATTACHMENT STYLES

While the evolutionary roots of anxious attachment provide an overarching framework, a child's individual experiences with caregivers significantly shape their attachment style. Children develop secure attachments when they experience consistent and responsive caregiving. This means that their caregivers quickly and reliably meet their needs, responding appropriately to their cries and signals. When children feel they can depend on their caregivers, they develop trust, forming the foundation of secure attachment.

However, children may develop an anxious attachment style when caregiving is inconsistent or neglectful. When a child's needs are met sporadically or unpredictably, the child becomes hyper-vigilant and constantly seeks reassurance, fearing abandonment. These behaviors are adaptive responses to the early experiences of unreliable caregiving.

For example, suppose a caregiver is affectionate and responsive at times but distant or unavailable at other times. In that case, it creates a confusing environment for the child. This inconsistency makes relationships feel unpredictable and unreliable, leading to the development of anxious attachment. Conversely, children who experience consistent emotional support from caregivers are likelier to develop secure attachment styles.

Traumatic childhood experiences, such as emotional or physical abuse, can also significantly impact attachment. When caregivers are abusive or neglectful, children learn that the people who are supposed to provide love and safety may also cause pain and fear. This duality can create a turbulent internal world where love and anxiety become intertwined. Similarly, parental separation or loss can disrupt a child's sense of stability, leading to anxious behaviors in future relationships. A trauma-informed approach to anxiety attachment recovery with a therapist or counselor can be highly beneficial if this is the case.

Another critical factor is the transmission of attachment styles across generations. As the primary caregivers and role models, parents unconsciously pass down their attachment patterns to their children. For instance, a parent with anxious attachment may exhibit overprotective or inconsistent behaviors, which the child may internalize and model. This cycle of attachment behaviors can perpetuate anxious attachment across generations.

There is hope for adults who have developed anxious attachment patterns due to their childhood experiences. Inner child healing exercises offer a practical approach. They involve reconnecting with the wounded inner child and providing the nurturing missed during childhood. We will cover this inner healing in more depth in Chapter 4.

THE NEUROSCIENCE BEHIND ATTACHMENT STYLES

Understanding the neuroscience that plays a pivotal part in attachment styles is essential. You will better understand why we act and feel the way we do in our relationships. Our brain wiring is a complex system that governs how we think, feel, and react, as well as the nature of our attachments. The amygdala is located deep within our brain. It is a small structure shaped like an almond, and it plays a fundamental role in how we process emotional responses. It becomes significantly activated when we are experiencing intense anxiety or fear, which can trigger a fight-or-flight response. When we feel an intense fear of abandonment, it is caused by our amygdala activating. Its purpose is to prepare our body to react to a perceived threat. This response has deep roots in our evolutionary past when we needed to react quickly to threats to survive.

Your prefrontal cortex is situated at the front of your brain. It carries out higher-order functions, such as emotional regulation, impulse control, and decision-making. This area also plays a part in letting us assess situations in a rational way and make logical decisions. If you are a person with anxious attachment, you have a weaker connection between the prefrontal cortex and the amygdala. This means it is harder to regulate your emotions during stressful moments. Also, you will be prone to overthinking and have trouble calming down if you feel there are threats to your relationship.

We often call oxytocin the "love hormone." It plays a significant role in bonding and attachment, and it is released during physical touch, such as hugging or holding hands. This hormone enhances feelings of trust and connection, which is crucial for establishing and maintaining strong bonds between people in relationships. If you have an anxious attachment style, the craving to have physical contact and reassurance is probably partially a result of craving oxytocin release. This biological drive helps us better understand how vital physical affection can be in forging secure attachments and reducing anxiety.

Other complex processes include the neurochemical interactions that form the basis for attachment and emotional responses. Dopamine and serotonin are neurotransmitters fundamental to mood regulation and emotional well-being. Dopamine is linked to pleasure and reward. It reinforces positive behaviors that make us feel good, such as spending time with loved ones. Serotonin is a little bit different. It focuses more on stabilizing our mood by helping us feel calm and happy. If you have an imbalance in these neurotransmitters, you will probably feel anxious and emotionally unstable. Both these emotions are significant in anxious attachment.

Additionally, stress hormones like cortisol play a role in responding to perceived threats. When cortisol levels increase, people tend to feel high levels of vigilance and anxiety. This makes it much harder for them to feel relaxed and have secure attachments.

Luckily, our brains have neuroplasticity, which allows them to reorganize and form new neural connections. This is a significant source of hope when changing our attachment patterns. We can rewire our brains by consciously adopting new thought patterns and behaviors. Our brains' adaptable nature helps us overcome anxious attachment styles and achieve security in our relationships. Treatment like cognitive behavioral therapy (CBT) can help reinforce these new neural pathways, promoting greater emotional regulation and stability.

As we have seen, neuroscience research has given us essential information on attachment styles. Brain imaging studies have demonstrated that people with different attachment styles show different brain activity patterns. As we have discussed, people with anxious attachment will often show heightened activity in the amygdala and lower connectivity with the prefrontal cortex. In longitudinal studies keeping track of people over time, it has been demonstrated how attachment-related brain changes tend to impact emotional and relational outcomes. It has also been found that specific genetic factors may make people more prone to particular attachment styles. However, environmental factors are highly significant.

I want you to understand that the neuroscience of attachment has practical implications for managing anxious attachment. If you have an anxious attachment style, one helpful strategy you can use to manage its effects is mindfulness practice. Practicing mindfulness can help calm your amygdala and strengthen the regulatory functioning of the prefrontal cortex, promoting better balance in your emotional responses. Neurofeedback is another therapeutic intervention that trains you to alter your brain activity.

It may help people with anxious attachments develop better emotional stability. Also, changing your lifestyle, such as getting enough sleep, eating healthy food, and regularly exercising, can support your brain health and may improve attachment security.

If you incorporate these strategies, you should be able to leverage your brain plasticity to develop healthier, more secure attachment patterns. Throughout this book, specifically in Chapter 3, we will explore these practical healing techniques, like CBT, mindfulness practices, and self-compassion exercises, in more depth—all effective in healing attachment wounds.

THE EMOTIONAL IMPACT OF ANXIOUS ATTACHMENT

If you have an anxious attachment style, you probably feel like you are living in a constant storm of emotions. You may be so frequently worried and fearful of abandonment that it is difficult to think or focus. You might experience intense anxiety just because there is a slight change in the tone of your partner's voice or a delay in a text message. You often feel on edge because you constantly fear being left alone. You have a constant feeling of insecurity in every part of your relationship.

There is even more emotional turmoil beyond that. For example, people with anxious attachments often experience dramatic emotional changes and mood swings. Intense emotional highs and lows leave you (and your partner) feeling drained and exhausted. Stability seems unattainable as you are in a perpetual state of emotional flux. You will find that your mental and physical well-being are negatively impacted over time.

Anxious attachment also commonly causes overthinking and obsessive thoughts about your relationship. You may replay past conversations, ruminating over every word and gesture, looking for hidden meanings. You might find it challenging to relax and sleep. Overthinking tends to cause anxiety, and you can end up in a vicious cycle that is difficult to break. I have struggled through this experience and know that your mind makes you feel like a prisoner, trapping you in an endless loop of anxiety and doubt. This makes it very challenging to enjoy the present moment or think positively about the future.

Before I took steps to address my anxious attachment, I found that it had a devastating impact on my self-esteem and sense of self-worth. One of the damaging aspects of frequently craving validation from others to have positive feelings about yourself is that your self-esteem becomes dependent on other people. This makes you too vulnerable to feelings of inadequacy and self-doubt, as you tend to believe you are inadequate when you are on your own. This might manifest in feeling inferior in social settings and underestimating your abilities. If you have this problem, you may negatively compare yourself to others and hold yourself back from trying new challenges.

Anxious attachment styles also put an enormous strain on relationships. The tendency toward jealousy and possessiveness can cause misunderstandings and conflict. A typical scenario is that you tend to be anxious about everything your partner does, seeing their interactions with other people as threats. When this kind of jealousy is present in a relationship, it can be toxic for both partners. Trust will erode, and it will likely cause an emotional distance. Many case studies have demonstrated how this kind of behavior can destroy the stability of a relationship, causing a cycle of conflict and reconciliation that will likely leave you feeling exhausted and disconnected.

You can do several different things to change these emotional responses and cultivate emotional security. You will find it easier to stay grounded and calm even during challenging moments when you use emotional regulation techniques. This involves methods such as deep breathing exercises and developing better self-compassion and self-care. Being kind to yourself and prioritizing your well-being means you can strengthen your sense of self-worth, so you are not depending on external validation. Mindfulness practices will also help you create better emotional resilience, making coping with anxiety and having more stable relationships much more manageable. We will thoroughly cover more detailed techniques and processes for long-term emotional stability throughout the rest of the book.

It takes a lot of work to achieve emotional security. It does not happen overnight. You must exert continual effort, be willing to face your fears, use the right strategies, and deeply consider how anxious attachment impacts you emotionally. In this way, you can start to transform your emotional responses. Making these changes means you can feel safe and secure in your relationships, with high trust and mutual support. You will create a feeling of peace within yourself and a sense of stability in your interpersonal interactions.

CHAPTER 2
IDENTIFYING ANXIOUS ATTACHMENT AND EMOTIONAL TRIGGERS

THERE WAS A TIME SEVERAL YEARS AGO WHEN I WAS CONSTANTLY feeling anxious and on edge. It felt like I was being tested every time I spoke to my partner. I was continually seeking reassurance that I would not lose their affection. On one occasion, there was a particularly intense argument. It plunged me into self-doubt. I could not understand why I would react so dramatically and always seemed to fear the worst. It only took a short amount of introspection to realize that I needed to understand myself for any chance of healing.

My goal in this chapter is to help you become self-aware. I will show you how to reveal the causes of your anxious attachment and suggest tools to identify and understand them so that you can manage them. As I mentioned in the previous chapter, exploring the source of anxious attachment may bring up traumatic events in your life. So, contact professional therapists or counselors if you need support.

SELF-IDENTIFYING AND UNDERSTANDING ANXIOUS ATTACHMENT

You need insight into your attachment style to achieve emotional health and personal growth, especially in relationships. I recommend using self-assessment tools to understand how you behave and respond emotionally.

You can start by doing online quizzes and assessments. If you look for these tools, stick to reputable psychology websites. When you take these quizzes, remember that they are designed to help you understand your current attachment style. They will usually ask several questions about your behaviors and emotions in relationships. For example, questionnaires may prompt you to reflect on your feelings and relationship behaviors. For instance, there might be questions such as "Do you often worry that your partner does not love you?" or "How frequently do you seek reassurance from your partner?" You may also be asked to reflect on your reactions when your partner does not respond to a message as quickly as you would like. Answering these questions honestly can provide a clearer picture of your attachment style.

The next step to take is interpreting your assessment results. Quizzes or formal inventories you take may give you a scoring method to categorize your attachment style. Make sure that you understand the score breakdowns. You might have an anxious attachment style if you get a high score on the fear of abandonment questions. It is helpful to compare your results with known attachment styles to get more insight. If you get an indication that you tend to have an anxious attachment, you then need to know about the behaviors and feelings linked to this style.

After that, you need to identify the areas where you can improve. Do you constantly feel like you need reassurance or have obstacles to trust? By focusing on these areas, you can improve your efforts to make specific changes.

Your fundamental transformation can begin by connecting your assessment results to your daily relationship patterns and behaviors. If you have an assessment that shows intense anxiety in relationships, you probably overthink everything your partner says and does, looking for constant validation. You can see illustrations of the dynamics at work by imagining specific scenarios. For example, if your partner is busy at work and does not send an immediate response to your texts, you may have an anxious attachment style if you feel worried that they do not care or are losing interest. You will see patterns you must address more efficiently by understanding how your assessment results link to your behavior.

There are also more reflective self-questionnaires you can do. One benefit is how they require reflection on emotions and behavior, thus assisting you in understanding your potential patterns and triggers. Some questions you might need to answer include, "What are your emotions when your partner is not around?" and "What are the biggest fears you tend to have in relationships?" When you answer these questions, you will achieve much better clarity in understanding your attachment style. A more in-depth option is an attachment-style inventory. If you go to a therapist, you will likely be asked to answer the questions for one of these. They are used to assess your attachment style. They ask about your childhood experiences and relationship history.

You could also consult a checklist of common anxious attachment behaviors as a quick reference. Some behaviors include the tendency to overthink and ruminate about your relationships. These checklists will help you recognize typical signs and symptoms of anxious attachment. As alluded to above, you probably show an excessive need for reassurance if you have this attachment style. For example, you might constantly look for validation from your partner, asking questions like, "Do you still love me?" or "Are you mad at me?" The root of this constant need for affirmation tends to be caused by a deep-seated fear of abandonment. There are various ways that this fear may manifest, such as imagining that neutral behavior means rejection or anxious feelings when a partner is not immediately available. You may replay conversations in your mind often, dissecting every word and action, looking for hidden meanings. You probably worry about potential problems in the relationship's future, even if there are no apparent issues.

Reflective journaling is another helpful practice for identifying anxious attachment, which prompts you to examine and deeply understand your experiences and emotions. For example, you could write using prompts such as "What tends to cause anxiety for you in relationships?" and "How do you react when you feel fearful of being abandoned?" Using these reflective questions will help increase your self-awareness. They can help you better understand your attachment style and uncover patterns by tracking your emotions and thoughts.

You can also do mirror exercises to reflect on your feelings and inner world. To do this, look at yourself in the mirror and have an honest conversation with yourself about your fears and insecurities. Doing this exercise is helpful with confronting your emotions and understanding them on a deeper level. You may also benefit from guided meditations to achieve better inner awareness. The main focus of these meditations is grounding yourself in the present moment and maintaining awareness of your thoughts without judgment. This helps you develop a more balanced and mindful approach to your emotions.

It is easier to see how anxious attachment can manifest in your life if we look at a few personal stories I have heard. Consider Emma, who has an anxious attachment style and, in the past, has experienced consistent anxiety in her relationships. She was constantly craving reassurance and feared that her partners would leave her, and, unfortunately, this often ended with her partners feeling pushed away and frustrated. Emma started to help herself with self-examination and therapy. These assisted her in realizing that she had an anxious attachment style, and she began to work on increasing her confidence and trust in relationships.

We see a similar story with John, who struggled with relationship trust issues. He frequently had difficulty believing that his partner had genuine affection and loyalty toward him. As a result of this lack of trust, John experienced anxiety, emotional distress, and constant arguing with his partner. It was through acknowledging that he had an anxious attachment style and getting the right kind of help that John eventually was able to feel more secure in his relationships, helping them become a healthier couple.

Do not consider recognizing your attachment style as labeling yourself. Identifying and understanding your attachment style and how it manifests in your life is essential to achieving greater insight and having healthier, more fulfilling relationships.

When you have an anxious attachment style, you often feel like there is a constant conflict between craving closeness and fearing loss. Using self-assessment tools, reflecting on personal stories, and doing reflective exercises can help you begin to understand and disengage from anxious attachment patterns. With this awareness, you will be much better able to take actionable steps, manage your attachment-related anxiety, and build lasting, more secure relationships.

PERSONAL ATTACHMENT HISTORY: MAPPING YOUR PAST

Another tool I have found helpful is to create an attachment timeline to give you crucial insights into how your past shapes how you feel and behave in the present. Begin by thinking about the significant events and relationships in your life. Think back to your earliest memories of connection and disconnection. Did you feel secure and loved at those times, or do you remember some neglect or inconsistency? When you pinpoint these events, it will be easier to see the big picture. Reflect on pivotal moments. These could be moving to a new city, your parents divorcing, or a new sibling being born. Each of these events can influence your sense of stability and security. Think about how you felt during events like this, and analyze the reasons for your feelings. You will understand how your attachment style developed when you map out your past like this.

Remember what I discussed earlier about how your childhood experiences with your caregivers enormously impact your future attachment style. Spend time contemplating your relationships with your parents or primary caregivers. Did they make you anxious or uncertain, or were they dependable and consistent? You also need to consider family dynamics. If you had an unpredictable or chaotic family environment, you may have high anxiety and hypervigilance today. Remember that early experiences affect how we feel and act in our relationships.

It is also crucial to analyze your past relationships. Consider your previous romantic and platonic relationships. What were your feelings and emotional state in those relationships? Did you have anxiety about abandonment and not being good enough? Keep an eye out for common themes and behaviors. You might notice a tendency to become overly dependent on your partners. You might also realize that you get jealous and insecure frequently. Patterns in the way you respond emotionally are essential to examine. When you have to face conflict, do you have an anxious reaction? Or do you usually withdraw and just shut down? By understanding these patterns, you will find it easier to understand what caused your anxious attachment.

You need to do a lot of introspection to heal from the attachment-related wounds of the past. CBT and other therapeutic approaches, such as EMDR (eye movement desensitization and reprocessing), can be incredibly effective. Using these kinds of therapies will support you in processing and reframing traumatic experiences. This will cut down on how much they impact your current life. You should also do self-compassion exercises. Be kind and compassionate in how you speak to yourself, especially when you are dealing with anxiety. This change in your self-talk can be transformational for your emotional well-being and self-esteem. I have also benefited from rewriting my narratives. Try not to see yourself as a victim of your past. Instead, think of yourself as a survivor who has used their experiences to learn and grow. Make this change in your perspective and empower yourself with confidence. This will make you more resilient.

EMOTIONAL TRIGGERS: IDENTIFYING AND UNDERSTANDING THEM

Thinking deeply about your experiences and reactions can help uncover the hidden emotional patterns of your anxious attachment style, increasing your self-awareness. It will also help you learn about the factors that trigger you in relationships.

An emotional trigger is something that leads to an intense emotional reaction. For example, you may see specific situations that cause insecurity or anxiety. It could also be a memory or event. If you have an anxious attachment, you will probably have triggers that cause you to feel insecure or fearful. If you have an anxious attachment, your triggers may be perceived rejection, criticism, or even minor instances of neglect. For example, if your partner seems distracted during a conversation, you might immediately fear that they are losing interest. These triggers can lead to heightened emotional responses such as anxiety, anger, or sadness, often out of proportion to the actual event. It is crucial to understand your triggers to know how they affect your emotional well-being and relationship dynamics.

There is an easy way you can begin to identify your triggers—by keeping a trigger journal. Every time you have a strong emotional reaction, write down the situation that caused it. Note the specifics, including what was said, where you were, and who was involved. Reflect on your past emotional reactions. Consider situations in which you experienced intense anxiety or fear. What was happening at the time? What thoughts were running through your mind? Also, attend to the physical and emotional responses you experience when exposed to these triggers. Know about the physical cues of being triggered. These could be a knot in your stomach, a racing heart, or a sense of impending doom.

After you have found out what your triggers are, it is time to manage them. You could also do self-soothing activities, such as taking a warm bath or listening to your favorite music. Doing mindfulness exercises can be helpful, as can doing relaxation exercises such as deep breathing, progressive muscle relaxation, and mindfulness meditation. These exercises can calm your nervous system and reduce the intensity of your emotional reactions. I also recommend using cognitive reframing techniques. This means that you change how you interpret the event that triggers you. If you get triggered because your partner does not immediately respond to a text, you can reframe your thought that they are ignoring you because they do not care, instead thinking they are probably too busy to respond. It is equally essential to develop effective coping mechanisms. For example, you could seek support from a trusted friend or start a new hobby. (The next chapter will review these strategies and techniques more thoroughly.)

Let's take a look at a specific example with Sarah, who tended to feel intense anxiety when her partner, Tom, did not immediately respond to her messages. It was because she kept a trigger journal that she was able to identify her anxiety getting out of control whenever Tom was busy with his work or out with his friends. When thinking about her childhood, she realized that her father's unavailability was the root cause of her anxious attachment style. She began using cognitive reframing. She told herself that Tom was not rejecting her when there was a delay in his response. Also, she made mindfulness practice part of her routine, which was vital to keeping her grounded. Her anxiety eventually decreased, and she felt safe and secure in her connection with her partner.

So, to begin with, let us set aside some time every day to reflect on your triggers and how you respond emotionally. Make a note of situations that gave rise to a strong emotional reaction, and consider why they may have had this effect.

CHAPTER 3
MANAGING ANXIETY AND EMOTIONAL REGULATION

THERE HAVE BEEN TIMES I HAVE WOKEN UP IN THE MIDDLE OF THE night, my heart pounding and thoughts racing. Before I knew how to deal with this, my worry would not disappear when I tried to calm myself. Do you ever have moments like this? Many of us have endured intense anxiety triggered by the fears of abandonment that come with feelings of insecurity in relationships.

Practical strategies for managing anxiety are a lifeline at times like these. In this next chapter, we will discuss tools that you can use to relieve your stress and regulate your emotions. We will then look at some more long-term maintenance and planning for emotional balance and create a daily anxiety management routine.

STRATEGIES AND TOOLS FOR ANXIETY RELIEF AND EMOTIONAL REGULATION

Think of this section as a toolkit to reach into when you have moments like the one mentioned above. We will review several techniques you can harness to help relieve your anxiety and regulate your emotions.

Self-Soothing Techniques for Immediate Relief

Self-soothing is comforting yourself when you are feeling stressed or anxious. This is a crucial skill for all of us, but it is especially essential if you have anxiety and an anxious attachment style. Self-soothing techniques will help regulate your emotions, reduce stress, and return you to calm.

When you self-soothe, you make yourself feel safe and secure within yourself. Self-soothing is finding ways to calm yourself mentally and physically when you cannot find any external reassurance. It plays a vital role in emotional regulation. You will not need constant reassurance from other people because you will be able to control your emotional responses. This feeling of independence will empower you and allow you to enjoy more stability and fulfillment in your relationships.

If you have an anxious attachment, there are many situations in which you need self-soothing. One example might be feeling anxious after disagreeing with your partner, and you can use self-soothing to help you calm down and achieve clarity of thought. If you have anxiety in social settings or when in uncertain circumstances, you can also use self-soothing techniques to get immediate relief and help you navigate those kinds of situations.

Here are some practical physical self-soothing strategies that you can try:

1. **Weighted Blankets**: These have become popular lately, and many people find them comforting. The blanket gives gentle pressure that mimics a comforting hug, promoting safety and calm. It is beneficial during moments of intense anxiety or when you are having trouble falling asleep.
2. **Warm Bath**: A warm bath is another fantastic way to soothe your body and mind. The warmth of the water can reduce your anxiety and relax your muscles. You could add a calming scent (lavender is a good choice) to your bath, making it even more relaxing.
3. **Light Exercise**: Another self-soothing method is light physical exercise, such as walking or gentle yoga. Exercise helps because it releases endorphins, which are natural mood lifters. Plus, it helps distract your mind from thoughts that are making you anxious.

Along with physical techniques, you can also use emotional self-soothing methods:

1. **Listening to Music**: One example is listening to some tranquil music. I find that this quickly transforms my mood to a more peaceful state, reducing anxiety and promoting relaxation. Make a playlist of calming songs and use it during stressful moments.

2. **Positive Affirmations**: I also recommend doing positive affirmations. When you use affirmations, you challenge negative thoughts and promote a more balanced perspective. Some helpful affirmations are "I am safe and loved," "I am capable of handling this," and "I trust the process of life." By repeating these affirmations, you will positively change your mindset and cut down on your anxiety.

3. **Creative Activities**: You can also try participating in creative activities such as drawing, painting, or writing. These activities are a healthy and productive outlet for emotional expression and can be a type of mindfulness practice, improving your focus.

I have found it helpful to have a personal self-soothing toolkit. It has made making self-soothing a part of my daily life much easier. Include items that make you feel happy and comforted, such as a journal, a blanket, or a book. I always keep my self-soothing toolkit nearby to use whenever I need to. Making time every day to do self-soothing activities can help to prevent anxiety before it starts. This could be a bit of deep breathing every morning or a relaxing bath at night.

As we see, self-soothing is helpful for people who suffer from the anxiety of anxious attachment. Knowing how to soothe yourself without needing help from anyone else can create calmer and more stable relationships.

Grounding Exercises for Anxiety and Emotional Stability

I have discovered that grounding exercises are practical for anxiety and emotion stabilization. Do grounding exercises to keep your mind in the present and connected to the here and now. Grounding has been able to anchor me when I have been otherwise overwhelmed by anxiety. When you ground yourself, you use your senses to secure your focus in the present. I know from experience that this can be an enormously helpful tool when you are anxious. Bring your focus to tangible, sensory experiences, and you will find that it helps you disrupt the cycle of worry, establishing better control over your emotional state.

Grounding has many benefits. One is that it reduces the immediate sense of panic, creating a sense of calm. Grounding can also be a mental and emotional reset button, letting you break free from the grip of anxious thoughts. Try grounding before situations that make you nervous, such as a big presentation at work or during an emotionally wrought conversation.

Here is one effective physical grounding technique: it is called the 5-4-3-2-1 technique. It engages all of your senses and makes you reconnect with your surroundings. You can practice it by identifying five things you can see around you. Next, focus on four things you can touch, followed by three things you can hear. After that, focus on two things you can smell and one thing you can taste. When you do this exercise, it helps to redirect your attention away from anxious thoughts and back to the present moment. Another surprisingly effective technique is holding an ice cube or other cold object. The intense sensation of cold can snap you out of an anxious state by forcing your focus on the physical sensation. Another way to ground yourself is to walk barefoot on grass. You will benefit from the soothing texture and coolness of the grass and feel more connected to the earth.

You could also try mental grounding techniques. One I often use is counting backward from 100. It requires focus and concentration, helping to distract your mind from anxiety. You can also try creating a detailed description of an object to help ground your thinking. Choose an object nearby and describe its size, shape, color, and texture. Doing this means you have to focus on something specific and tangible, and you will be pulled away from your anxious thoughts. Another approach is reciting a favorite poem or song. The rhythm and familiarity of the words can be calming, and as you focus on the recitation, you shift your attention away from the anxiety.

I recommend creating a grounding routine for yourself. It can help you make grounding exercises a part of your daily life. Decide on the specific times of each day when you will do grounding. This could be in the morning as you begin your day or in the evening when you want to relax. I recommend bringing together grounding techniques with other strategies for anxiety management. Here is an example. You could begin with a grounding exercise and follow it up with a mindfulness meditation or a breathing exercise. Doing grounding exercises in various environments to improve your adaptability is also helpful. I make sure that I have a repertoire of grounding techniques that can make it easier to manage anxiety wherever you find yourself.

As shown here, grounding techniques will help you manage your emotions when you have an anxious attachment style. If you understand how important it is to stay grounded and use mental and physical grounding exercises in your routine, you will create a better feeling of stability. This will help you stay calm when your anxiety starts to rise. I recommend developing a consistent grounding routine, empowering you to deal with your anxious attachment more effectively.

Visualization Practices to Calm the Mind

Visualization is also a great idea, as it is a powerful tool for managing anxiety. It gives you psychological and physiological benefits that may dramatically alleviate your stress. Engaging in visualization means you use your mind to create calming and peaceful images that help to reduce your heart rate and muscle tension. There is science behind this technique. It is based on how visualization can activate the same neural pathways as real experiences. When you vividly imagine a peaceful scene, you get a brain response similar to being in that environment. This means that calm neurotransmitters like dopamine and serotonin are released. Visualization is an incredibly fantastic tool when you are in a high-stress situation. This could be before a big meeting, during a confrontation, or even when you feel overwhelmed by daily tasks. You will have a mental escape, allowing you to regain control over your emotions and thoughts.

The most important part of visualization is guided imagery exercises. One of the most effective exercises is to visualize a peaceful place. Close your eyes and picture a comfortable, quiet place encouraging a tranquil mind. This could be a beach, a forest, or a cozy room. Take the time to imagine and picture all the details. Imagine all the sensory input you would experience if you visualized the beach. This includes the sound of waves crashing and the feel of the sand under your feet. This can become a mental sanctuary to which you can retreat whenever you get anxious. Another helpful exercise you can try when you are feeling anxiety is imagining a positive outcome to whatever stressful situation you may be in. Are you worried about giving a presentation at work? Visualize yourself speaking confidently and receiving positive feedback, as well as the feeling of being accomplished. Using this positive imagery can have an enormous impact on reducing anxiety and building confidence. You can also create a mental sanctuary for relaxation. Design a space in your mind where you can retreat whenever anxiety strikes. You can imagine a range of comforting objects in it, such as soft pillows, calming colors, and soothing sounds.

You can integrate practical visualization techniques into your daily life with ease. I find the "safe place" visualization highly effective in many situations. Whenever you feel anxious, close your eyes and picture a place where you feel completely safe and secure. Examples could be a childhood home, a favorite vacation spot, or even an imaginary world. It is also good to visualize success in challenging situations. Whenever you need to face a difficult task, visualize yourself achieving success for a few moments. Picture yourself meeting the challenge head-on, succeeding, getting praise, and feeling proud. In my experience, this technique is great for boosting confidence and reducing anxiety. Also, mindful visualization is something you can try, especially when you are doing everyday activities. For example, while washing your dishes, imagine the water washing away your stress. Or perhaps while walking, you could visualize each step grounding you and bringing you closer to a calm state.

Think about using visualization apps and tools. Some out there provide guided exercises, which are great for reminding you to practice regularly. Many apps or videos with guided visualizations can be highly effective. They offer a variety of guided visualizations tailored to different needs. I recommend combining visualization with other relaxation techniques to make it even more effective. For instance, I usually begin with deep breathing to relax before I start my visualization.

With the proper visualization practices, you have a robust and accessible way to manage your anxiety. By understanding the benefits and science behind visualization, engaging in guided imagery exercises, and incorporating practical techniques into your daily routine, you can create a mental toolkit for reducing stress and enhancing emotional well-being. With visualization, you can make a mental sanctuary, a place where you can find peace and calm amid the chaos of daily life, helping you navigate challenges with greater ease and confidence.

Breathing Exercises for Reducing Stress and Emotional Regulation

Do breathing exercises to manage your stress and anxiety. Breathing is so powerful because it affects your body's physiological responses. Deep breathing techniques, for example, can activate your parasympathetic nervous system, helping to calm your body and reduce the fight-or-flight response. Controlled breathing can lower your heart rate, ease muscle tension, and promote relaxation. Breathing techniques are also helpful for emotional regulation in general.

1. **Diaphragmatic Breathing**: Also known as belly breathing, this is a simple yet effective method of calming one's mind. Breathing deeply into one's diaphragm activates the parasympathetic nervous system, encouraging relaxation. This technique can help reduce anxiety, lower stress levels, and bring a sense of calm. Begin by sitting or lying down in a comfortable position. Put one hand on your chest and the other on your belly. Take a deep breath through your nose so your belly rises as air fills your lungs. Your chest should remain relatively still. Do a slow exhale through your mouth, allowing your belly to fall. Repeat these steps several times over several minutes, focusing on the rise and fall of your belly. This technique helps deepen your breath and promote relaxation.

2. **Resonant Breathing**: Also referred to as coherent breathing, this technique involves breathing at a rate that maximizes your heart rate variability, which may promote relaxation and emotional stability. When you want to practice resonant breathing, sit or lie comfortably, slowly inhale through your nose for a few seconds, and then slowly exhale through your nose. Aim to maintain a steady, even rhythm, breathing at about five deep, slow breaths per minute. This technique tends to be effective for synchronizing your heart rate and breathing, reducing stress and anxiety.

3. **4-7-4 Breathing**: This is another powerful breathing technique to reduce anxiety. Start by sitting or lying down

and getting yourself comfortable. Close your eyes, and then inhale quietly through your nose. Hold for a few seconds. After that, exhale completely through your mouth for a count of eight. This extended exhalation helps you expel more air from your lungs, promoting a sense of calm. Repeat this cycle three to four times, allowing yourself to relax with each breath.

4. **Box Breathing**: Also known as square breathing, this is a technique that Navy SEALs use to stay calm and focused even in the most high-pressure situations. Here is how to practice box breathing. Sit comfortably with your back straight, and then close your eyes. Inhale slowly through your nose. Try to hold your breath for a count of four. Exhale slowly through your mouth. Finally, try to hold your breath again for a count of four. Repeat this cycle four to five times, maintaining a steady rhythm. Using this technique may help you get control over your breathing, reducing anxiety.

5. **Alternate Nostril Breathing**: Try this advanced breathing technique to achieve a deeper level of relaxation. Alternate nostril breathing, also called *Anulom Vilom*, is a practice yoga practitioners use to balance the mind and body. Sit in a comfortable position, keeping your spine straight. Using your right thumb, close your right nostril and inhale deeply through the left. Then, close your left nostril with your ring finger and release the right one, exhaling fully through the right. Inhale through the right nostril, close it with your thumb, then exhale through the left nostril. Keep repeating this pattern for several minutes, focusing on

your breath. This technique can make me feel more balanced and calmer.

6. **Breath-Counting Meditations**: I also like doing a combination of breathwork and meditation. It is another advanced technique that combines mindfulness and controlled breathing. Start sitting comfortably with a straight back, then close your eyes. Take a few deep breaths and take your time settling in. After that, breathe naturally and start counting each exhale. Count "one" on the first exhale, "two" on the next, and so on. Keep going until you get to five. After reaching five, start over at one. If your mind wanders, gently bring your focus back to your breath and the counting. With this technique, you will stay present and centered, alleviating your anxious thoughts.

Breathing exercises can significantly reduce stress and anxiety in daily life. Therefore, creating reminders to practice breathing exercises at different points of the day can be beneficial. For example, you could do your breathing exercises in the morning, during your lunch break, or before bed. Combining your breathing exercises with mindfulness and meditation will make them even more centering and calming. For instance, you could begin with a breathing exercise to calm your mind, and after that, you could do a mindfulness meditation to keep yourself in the present moment. Remember that once you know how to do breathing exercises, you can do them in various situations, such as at home, work, or public places. When you have a repertoire of breathing techniques, they can empower you to manage anxiety wherever you are.

Cognitive-Behavioral Techniques for Anxiety Management

CBT is established to be one of the best methods of anxiety management. With CBT, you focus on noticing and changing your negative thought patterns that cause you anxiety and distress. It is based on interconnectedness regarding your feelings, thoughts, and behaviors. Addressing irrational and unhelpful thinking patterns can positively influence your emotions and behavior. CBT is especially beneficial for people with anxious attachment, as it offers practical methods for challenging your worried thoughts, giving you a way to reframe them. By taking part in CBT therapy, you get empowered to get the control you need over your anxiety. This gives you a way to improve your psychological health and the health of your relationships.

When you do CBT, one of the first steps you will take is identifying your negative thought patterns. In CBT, these patterns are called cognitive distortions. They include common pitfalls, such as catastrophizing. That is when you imagine the worst possible outcome or engage in black-and-white thinking, where you see situations in extremes without understanding that there are gray areas and middle ground. You could write in a thought diary, a powerful tool for this purpose; every time you start feeling anxious, write down the situation, what you think about it, and the emotions resulting from your thoughts. There are specific questions you can ask yourself for reflection. For example, ask yourself, "What evidence do I have for this thought?" or "Is there another way to interpret this situation?" When you ask yourself to answer these questions, you are encouraged to think critically about how you tend to react.

After you have noticed your negative thoughts, you need to do cognitive restructuring. Doing this process means that you challenge and change your negative thoughts. Begin by contemplating the evidence for and against your anxious thoughts. An example could be if you think, "My partner did not call me, so they must be losing interest," seek evidence that contradicts this thought, such as when your partner has shown you care and affection. You should also try positively reframing your thoughts. For instance, instead of thinking, "They did not call because they do not care," you might reframe this thought as "They are likely busy but will call when they can." By practicing using alternative, balanced thinking, you get practice consistently applying your new, more rational thoughts so much that they will eventually become second nature.

CBT involves a combination of behavioral techniques and cognitive strategies. Exposure exercises allow you to face your fears with a controlled and gradual approach. Do you fear being alone? You might begin by spending short periods alone, gradually stepping up the time as you become more comfortable. You can even try to do behavioral experiments to help you test the validity of your negative thoughts. Let's take a look at an example. Say that you believe asking for reassurance would annoy your partner; try asking them about this calmly and carefully and see what reaction you get. Doing this can give you real-life evidence that contradicts your fears. This kind of exercise provides gradual desensitization, which means slowly exposing yourself to situations that cause anxiety to cut down on your sensitivity over time. Do social situations cause stress for you?

Begin by attending small gatherings and gradually working up to more significant events.

LONG-TERM MAINTENANCE FOR EMOTIONAL REGULATION AND BALANCE

Life can be overwhelming for anyone, but it tends to be even more distressing for people with anxious attachments. That is why self-awareness and emotional regulation are so vitally important. Emotional regulation is managing and healthily responding to one's emotional experiences. It is an essential tool for navigating life's ups and downs with greater ease and resilience.

You need solid emotional regulation for good mental health and healthy relationships. Effective emotional dysregulation means regulating your emotions even in the most distressing conditions. This is crucial, as emotional dysregulation can lead to impulsive actions, strained relationships, and mental health issues. Emotional dysregulation occurs when you have intense emotional responses disproportionate to the situation—for example, feeling overwhelming anger over a minor inconvenience or experiencing deep sadness from a slight criticism.

These intense emotional reactions can disrupt your life, making it hard to maintain stable relationships and a sense of well-being. Regularly developing better emotional regulation skills can enhance your emotional intelligence, improve your relationships, and foster a sense of inner peace.

Regular Mindfulness and Breathing Practices for Self-Awareness

When you are mindful, you are fully present in the moment and aware of your thoughts, feelings, and surroundings without judgment. It is about paying attention to the here and now rather than getting lost in past regrets or future worries. You will enhance your self-awareness by improving your mindfulness, as it helps you notice your emotional and physical reactions as they happen. This awareness can improve emotional regulation, stress reduction, and mental health. Practicing mindfulness regularly can help you develop a deeper understanding of your inner world, making it easier to manage your emotions and respond to life's challenges with greater clarity and calm.

Practicing mindfulness regularly has many other benefits, including reducing anxiety and stress. When you practice mindfulness, you create a space between yourself and your reactions, letting you observe your thoughts and emotions without them overwhelming you. This detachment can help you respond more thoughtfully rather than react impulsively. Mindfulness can also improve focus and concentration, enhance self-compassion, and promote inner peace. Examples of mindfulness practices include mindful breathing, body scan meditation, and mindful observation of daily activities. Each of these practices offers a unique way to cultivate awareness and presence.

Mindful breathing exercises are a cornerstone of mindfulness practice. As we discussed earlier, focused breathing techniques involve paying close attention to your breath, feeling the air fill your lungs, and noticing the rise and fall of your chest. If your mind wanders, gently bring your attention back to your breath. Counting breaths can also enhance mindfulness. Inhale deeply and count "one," then exhale and count "two." Continue counting with each breath until you reach ten, then start over. This simple exercise can help anchor your mind and increase your awareness of the present moment.

Breathing with body awareness takes mindful breathing a step further by focusing on physical sensations. As you breathe in, notice how the air feels as it enters your nose, travels down your throat, and fills your lungs. Pay attention to the subtle movements in your body as you breathe, such as the expansion of your rib cage and the gentle rise of your abdomen. On the exhale, notice the sensation of the breath leaving your body and the slight relaxation that follows. With this practice, you will connect more deeply with your body. It can be exceptionally grounding and calming.

Another tool to use for self-awareness is body scan meditation. This practice involves mentally scanning your body from head to toe, paying attention to any sensations you notice. The first step is to find a comfortable position and close your eyes. Begin to relax by taking a few deep breaths. Start by focusing on the top of your head and slowly move your attention down your body. Notice any areas of tension, discomfort, or relaxation. Observe your feelings rather than trying to change anything. For example, you might feel tightness in your shoulders or warmth in your hands. Reflecting on these physical sensations can help you become more attuned to your body and its signals. A guided body scan meditation script can further assist in this practice, providing step-by-step instructions to help you stay focused and present.

Use mindful observation to understand your surroundings and internal states without judgment. Observe each thought and emotion as it arises, refraining from labeling it good or bad. For instance, if you notice a feeling of sadness, acknowledge it by saying to yourself, "I am feeling sad," without trying to push it away or analyze it. This non-judgmental awareness can help you develop a more accepting and compassionate relationship with yourself. Mindful observation can also be applied to daily activities. Whether you are washing dishes, walking, or eating, try to engage in the experience fully. Notice the sights, sounds, smells, and sensations involved in the activity. This practice can transform mundane tasks into opportunities for mindfulness and presence.

Reflective questions can further enhance your practice of mindful observation. Ask yourself, "What thoughts and emotions am I experiencing right now?" or "How do my surroundings affect my mood?" These questions encourage you to explore your inner world and deepen your self-awareness. Regular practice of mindful observation lets you develop a greater sense of presence and clarity, making it easier to navigate life's challenges with a calm and balanced mind.

Self-Compassion Exercises

Self-compassion is a necessary part of emotional regulation and overall well-being. It means you treat yourself with the kindness and understanding you would offer a close friend. It involves acknowledging your suffering without judgment and recognizing that imperfection is a shared human experience. There are profound benefits to showing yourself compassion. It can reduce your anxiety, increase resilience, and improve your overall mental health. Let's take a look at an example. Imagine you have made a mistake at work. Instead of criticizing yourself, you might acknowledge that everyone makes mistakes and use them as learning opportunities. This shift in perspective can lead to better emotional balance and greater self-acceptance.

I like taking self-compassion breaks. They are a practical way to incorporate this practice into your daily life. When you notice stress or self-criticism, pause and give yourself a moment of kindness. Start by acknowledging your suffering. You might say, "This is hard right now." Next, remind yourself that suffering is a part of life, saying, "I am not alone; others feel this way too." Finally, offer yourself a kind gesture, such as placing a hand over your heart and saying, "May I be kind to myself." Reflecting on your need for self-compassion can help you recognize when you are being too harsh with yourself. Practice scenarios for self-compassion breaks could include moments of failure, rejection, or intense pressure. Take regular self-compassion breaks to create a more compassionate relationship with yourself.

Self-compassionate journaling is another effective tool. Start by using journaling prompts focused on self-compassion. For example, write about a time when you struggled and how you responded to yourself. Reflect on whether you were kind or critical. Another prompt might be to list ways to be more compassionate with yourself in the future. It is equally important to reflect on your self-critical thoughts. Notice when you are being harsh with yourself and challenge these thoughts. For instance, if you think, "I am not good enough," ask yourself if this is accurate and what evidence you have to support it. Writing letters to yourself with compassion can also be powerful. Treat yourself like you would a dear friend, providing words of kindness and encouragement. This exercise can help shift your inner dialogue from critical to supportive.

Another technique I like to use is compassionate imagery. In this approach, you visualize a compassionate figure offering kindness and support. Begin by finding a quiet place to sit comfortably. Close your eyes and take a few deep breaths. Visualize a person who embodies compassion. This could be someone you know, a historical figure, or even an imagined being. Imagine this person offering you warmth and kindness. Imagine them saying words of comfort and understanding. Reflect on the feelings evoked by this imagery. You might feel a sense of relief, warmth, or connection. Compassionate imagery can support you during stressful times, offering a mental refuge of kindness and empathy.

Make self-compassion exercises part of your daily life so that you will foster a more nurturing and supportive relationship with yourself. Whether taking self-compassion breaks, journaling, or using compassionate imagery, each practice offers a way to cultivate kindness and understanding. Shifting your perspective in this way can bring you better emotional balance, resilience, and overall well-being. Self-compassion allows you to transform your inner dialogue and create a foundation of support and kindness that enhances every aspect of your life.

Cognitive Reappraisal and Emotional Labeling

Cognitive reappraisal is a technique that involves changing the way you interpret and respond to situations. You can change your emotional response when you reinterpret a problem from a different perspective. The steps for cognitive reappraisal include identifying the negative thought, challenging its validity, and replacing it with a more balanced perspective. For example, if you receive critical feedback at work, your initial reaction might be to feel hurt and defensive. By practicing cognitive reappraisal, you can reframe the feedback as an opportunity for growth and improvement. By making this kind of shift in perspective, you can reduce negative emotions and promote a more positive outlook.

You can practice this kind of cognitive reappraisal by doing reflective exercises. Begin by noting a recent situation that triggered a strong emotional response. Identify the specific negative thoughts you had about the problem. Present a challenge to these thoughts by asking yourself questions such as, "Is there evidence to support this thought?" or "Could there be another explanation?" Finally, reframe the situation with a more balanced perspective. For example, if you felt rejected because a friend canceled plans, you might reframe it by considering that they might have had a legitimate reason and still value your friendship. Regular cognitive reappraisal can help you develop a more resilient and balanced approach to life's challenges.

You can also become skilled in emotional labeling to achieve sound emotional regulation. This means that you learn how to recognize and name your emotions accurately. After all, you need to know your feelings before genuinely understanding and managing them. The importance of emotional labeling lies in its ability to provide clarity and reduce the intensity of negative emotions. When you accurately label your feelings, your prefrontal cortex is activated. This helps you regulate the emotional response generated by the amygdala. This process can create a sense of distance from the emotion, allowing you to respond more thoughtfully.

To practice emotional labeling, tune into your physical sensations and thoughts. Ask yourself, "What am I feeling right now?" and try to identify the specific emotion. It might be anger, sadness, fear, or frustration. Use precise words to describe the feeling, such as "annoyed" instead of "angry" or "disappointed" instead of "sad." Journaling prompts can also aid in emotional labeling. For instance, write about a recent event and describe the emotions you felt during and after the event. Reflect on how these emotions influenced your thoughts and actions. Regularly practicing emotional labeling can enhance your emotional awareness and regulation skills.

You should incorporate these techniques into your daily life to significantly improve your ability to regulate emotions. Whether you practice cognitive reappraisal or emotional labeling, each method is valuable for managing your emotional experiences. These skills can help you navigate the complexities of relationships and life with greater ease and resilience, fostering a sense of emotional balance and well-being.

Guided Meditations for Emotional Balance

Guided meditations are structured practices where a narrator, often in a soothing voice, leads you through a series of steps to achieve a specific mental state. These meditations help you focus your thoughts, calm your mind, and achieve emotional balance. You can use guided meditations to support your emotional regulation by giving you a framework for calming your thoughts and directing your attention inward. They can reduce stress, increase self-awareness, and promote peace. Examples of guided meditations include loving-kindness meditation, grounding meditation, and emotional release meditation. Each offers unique benefits, and you can tailor them to your needs.

Loving-kindness meditation (*metta* meditation) fosters compassion for yourself and others. To do this practice, you need to silently repeat (in your mind or whispering) phrases that convey goodwill and kindness. To begin, find a quiet place to sit comfortably. Close your eyes and take a few deep breaths. Start by directing loving-kindness toward yourself. Silently repeat phrases such as, "May I be happy. May I be healthy. May I be safe. May I live with ease." Next, extend these wishes to someone you care about, repeating similar phrases. Gradually include a neutral person, someone you struggle with, and all living beings. Doing this meditation is excellent for softening your heart and building greater empathy. As you reflect on the experience, you will probably notice a warm, tender feeling that grows with each repetition. This will enhance your sense of connection and compassion.

Use grounding meditation to help you stay present and balanced, especially during stressful times. It involves visualizing yourself firmly rooted in the ground, much like a tree with deep roots. Start by sitting in a comfortable position and closing your eyes. Take a few deep breaths to relax. Imagine roots growing from the soles of your feet, traveling deep into the earth. Visualize these roots anchoring you, providing stability and strength. Feel the connection with the ground beneath you, supporting you entirely.

Practical applications of this meditation include using it before a stressful event, like a presentation or difficult conversation, to help you remain calm and centered. The visualization of being deeply rooted can provide stability and resilience.

Emotional release meditation is a technique for letting go of pent-up emotions. In this practice, you can release emotions in a safe and controlled way. Begin by finding a comfortable position and close your eyes. Take several deep breaths to center yourself. Identify the emotion you wish to release, such as anger, sadness, or frustration. Visualize this emotion as a physical object within your body, such as a dark cloud or a heavy stone. With each exhale, imagine this object slowly dissolving or being expelled from your body. Techniques for visualizing emotional release include seeing the emotion dissipate into the air or flow away like water. As you reflect on the experience, you may feel a sense of lightness and relief as the emotional burden lifts, leaving you with a clear and calmer mind.

Guided meditations provide a structured approach to achieving emotional balance, and each type is best for specific needs. Whether you are fostering compassion through loving-kindness, finding stability with grounding techniques, or releasing pent-up emotions, these practices can transform your emotional landscape. Make guided meditations part of your routine to improve your emotional well-being and cultivate a more profound sense of inner peace.

The Role of Self-Care in Emotional Regulation

Self-care is taking deliberate actions to maintain and improve your physical, emotional, and mental well-being. It is about recognizing and meeting your needs, even when your life is busiest. Prioritizing self-care gives you a foundation for better emotional regulation. This means you are better equipped to handle stress, anxiety, and other emotional challenges. Think of self-care as recharging your internal batteries. Without it, you may run on empty, making you more likely to end up with emotional dysregulation and burnout.

Self-care offers many benefits when it comes to emotional regulation. Doing regular self-care will reduce your stress, improve your mood, and increase your resilience. For instance, engaging in activities that bring you joy, such as reading a book, walking in nature, or spending time with loved ones, can boost your mood and buffer against stress. Physical self-care activities, such as regular exercise, adequate sleep, and a balanced diet, can also profoundly affect your emotional well-being. When your body feels good, your mind often follows. Emotional self-care, like journaling, talking to a friend, or practicing gratitude, helps you process and manage your feelings. Mental self-care, such as setting boundaries, taking breaks, and engaging in hobbies, ensures you have the mental space to think clearly and make thoughtful decisions.

Creating a self-care plan begins with identifying your self-care needs and preferences. Everyone has different needs, so reflecting on what activities help you feel more balanced and rejuvenated is essential. Start by listing activities that you enjoy and that help

47

you achieve a sense of inner peace. These could be simple activities such as having a hot bath, doing yoga, and listening to your favorite music. After that, think about balancing different types of self-care. Physical self-care might include regular exercise, a healthy diet, and sufficient sleep. Emotional self-care could involve talking to a therapist, journaling, or practicing mindfulness. Mental self-care might encompass setting boundaries, taking mental health days, and engaging in creative hobbies. Make sure that you set realistic self-care goals. Aim for small, achievable goals that fit into your daily routine. For example, you might set a goal to take a ten-minute walk daily or spend fifteen minutes journaling each evening.

It takes intentionality and planning to make self-care part of your daily life. Start by scheduling your self-care activities like you would an appointment. For instance, you might block time in your calendar for a weekly yoga class or a daily meditation session. Combining self-care with other daily tasks can make it more manageable. You might practice deep breathing exercises while commuting, listen to calming music while cooking, or take a walk during your lunch break. Making self-care a nonnegotiable priority is essential. This means committing to your self-care activities even when life gets busy. It might help to remind yourself that taking care of your needs allows you to be more present and effective in other areas of your life.

You should evaluate your self-care practices continually, making adjustments when you need to do so to keep them aligned with your needs. I like keeping a self-care journal. It is perfect for tracking my self-care activities and reflecting on how they make me feel. I recommend that you keep a self-care journal, too. You can write down your reflections on how different self-care activities affect you to determine which ones work best. For instance, note any changes in your mood or energy levels after a week of regular exercise. Adjustments based on personal needs and feedback are a continuous process. Your self-care needs will change and evolve as your life circumstances change. So, take the time to reassess your self-care plan regularly and be flexible in adapting it to your current situation. This might mean trying new activities, increasing the frequency of specific practices, or letting go of activities that no longer serve you.

Self-care is a dynamic and ongoing practice critical to emotional regulation and well-being. By understanding your self-care needs, creating a balanced plan, integrating it into your daily life, and regularly evaluating its effectiveness, you can build a sustainable self-care routine that supports your emotional health and resilience.

Managing Emotional Volatility and Handling Emotional Triggers in Relationships

Emotional volatility can feel like riding a roller coaster with unpredictable highs and lows. It affects your well-being and relationships, leaving you exhausted and overwhelmed. Emotional volatility is characterized by intense and frequent emotional shifts that various factors can trigger. These triggers might include stress, unresolved trauma, relationship conflicts, or even minor daily inconveniences. For instance, a slight disagreement with a partner might escalate into a full-blown argument, or an offhand comment from a colleague could lead to a day of feeling upset and distracted. In daily life, emotional volatility tends to create significant problems with maintaining stable relationships, not to mention a sense of inner peace.

Building emotional resilience is critical to handling emotional volatility more effectively. Begin by recognizing areas where you can build resilience, such as stress management, self-care improvement, and relationships. Reflective exercises can help you develop resilience. For instance, keep a journal to document challenging situations and how you responded. Reflect on what worked well and what did not, and think about how you can apply these lessons in the future. Examples of resilient behaviors include maintaining a positive outlook, seeking solutions rather than dwelling on problems, and staying flexible in the face of change. Developing these habits can make you more adaptable and better equipped to handle and reduce emotional volatility.

As we saw at the end of Chapter 2, emotional triggers can significantly impact those with anxious attachment styles, often leading to heightened feelings of insecurity and fear of abandonment in relationships. Understanding and managing these triggers is crucial for recovery and fostering healthier connections. Here is a quick checklist summarizing critical points we have discussed in this chapter that will help you handle both emotional volatility and emotional triggers:

1. **Self-Awareness**: The first step in managing emotional volatility and triggers is recognizing them. You should take the time to identify specific situations, behaviors, or comments that evoke intense emotions. Journaling or

reflecting on past experiences can help you better understand your triggers and associated feelings.

2. **Grounding Techniques**: When faced with emotional volatility or triggers, grounding techniques can be incredibly effective in managing anxiety. These include deep breathing exercises, mindfulness practices, or physical activities that help redirect focus away from overwhelming emotions. Such techniques can create a sense of calm and help regain control over emotional responses.

3. **Coping Strategies**: Establishing coping strategies tailored to your needs is crucial. This process of self-discovery and self-care empowers individuals, giving them a sense of control over their emotional responses. This may include self-soothing techniques, affirmations, or engaging in hobbies that bring joy and comfort. Having a toolkit of coping strategies can empower us and reduce the impact of emotional triggers when they arise.

4. **Reframing Negative Thoughts**: Many with an anxious attachment may fall into patterns of negative thinking when confronted with triggers. Practicing cognitive restructuring, like CBT and cognitive reappraisal, can help shift perspective and diminish anxiety. Take time to challenge and reframe negative thoughts with more balanced thinking. Focusing on the positive aspects of our relationships can counteract fear and doubt and alter your emotional response, reducing the intensity of your reactions.

5. **Partner Communication**: After triggers are identified, it is vital to communicate openly with partners. Sharing what

triggers feelings of anxiety or insecurity can create a mutually supportive environment where both partners can work together to mitigate these triggers. This open dialogue fosters trust and understanding, which are essential to any healthy relationship. We will discuss the best communication techniques with our partners in Chapters 6 and 7.

6. **Gradual Exposure**: For triggers that frequently arise within specific scenarios, gradually exposing oneself to these situations can build resilience. This incremental approach allows us to face our fears in a controlled manner, helping to reduce anxiety over time and strengthen emotional responses.

7. **Support Systems**: These play a crucial role in managing emotional volatility. Identifying and contacting a support network can give you the emotional backing you need. This network might include friends, family, or support groups. Regular check-ins with people you trust can offer a space to express your feelings and gain perspective. An example could be having a weekly coffee date with a close friend or attending a weekly support meeting.

8. **Professional Support**: Make sure that you get professional help if you need it. Experienced counselors can be a game-changer for those struggling to manage emotional triggers. Therapy is a safe space to explore underlying issues associated with anxious attachment and develop specific coping strategies. A therapist can help us understand our triggers and foster healthier relational dynamics. They can also offer strategies tailored to your

needs and help you navigate particularly challenging periods of emotional volatility.

By employing these strategies, those of us with anxious attachment can begin to navigate our emotional volatility and triggers more effectively, facilitating recovery and promoting healthier, more secure relationships. Using the proper strategies to stabilize your emotions, build resilience, and leverage support systems can create more balance and peace in your emotional life. These strategies improve your well-being, making connecting with others in meaningful ways easier.

As you continue to explore these techniques, you will find that managing emotional triggers and volatility becomes more intuitive and less daunting, paving the way for deeper self-awareness and emotional stability. Emphasizing the need for self-compassion and patience throughout this journey is essential. It is important to remember that healing and growth take time, and being patient with yourself is okay as you work through these strategies.

Developing a Daily Anxiety Management Routine

It is best to have a structured anxiety management routine. When you have a routine, it helps to provide stability and predictability. This gives you comfort when you are feeling overwhelmed. When you know precisely what you will do each day to manage your anxiety, you gain a sense of certainty. This is important, as uncertainty is one of the primary triggers of anxiety. When you achieve consistency in your activities, your mind and body will more easily find a rhythm, making it easier to cope with stress. To create a positive tone, many people find it helpful to start their day with a set morning routine that includes mindfulness exercises. Ending each day with a calming routine that encourages sound sleep and overall well-being can also be helpful.

To create a personalized anxiety management routine, you must identify critical activities and exercises you feel will be most effective. You can start by listing the techniques you think will be most helpful, such as grounding, breathing, or cognitive restructuring. Once you have done that, think about your daily schedule and identify pockets of time you can most easily incorporate these activities. Remember the importance of balance. It is vital to make your routine flexible enough to accommodate unexpected daily changes. That way, you will not feel stressed if you need to make some adjustments or miss one of your sessions.

It is best to integrate a variety of anxiety management techniques into your routine to achieve a holistic approach that addresses multiple aspects of anxiety. For example, begin your morning by centering yourself with a grounding exercise. After that, do cognitive restructuring exercises to challenge negative thoughts. Throughout the day, use self-soothing techniques whenever you have feelings of anxiety, incorporating visualization practices to maintain a calm mindset.

To achieve long-term success, you must keep track of your routine, adjusting it whenever needed. Maintain a routine diary in which you track your activities and write down how they affect your anxiety levels. Use this record to think about what works well for you and what does not in reducing your anxiety—that way, you know what kinds of adjustments to make. If you discover a less effective technique, try using a different one. Review your routine regularly so you can make changes that keep your practices tailored to your needs. With this ongoing evaluation, staying engaged and motivated to keep up your routine for the long term is more manageable.

Create a well-rounded routine, including grounding, breathing, cognitive, and visualization techniques. That will give you the tools and stability to deal with everyday stressors. You will be empowered to take control of your anxiety, fostering greater emotional resilience and well-being. I also recommend combining cognitive and behavioral techniques to help you create a robust anxiety management framework. Identifying and restructuring negative thoughts and using behavioral strategies to reinforce positive changes can help you develop a more balanced and less anxious mindset. If you use this approach, you will probably find that it enables you to manage your anxiety immediately and builds long-term resilience and emotional stability.

Building Self-Trust

I want to end this chapter by mentioning that cultivating self-trust is a foundational element in recovering from anxious attachment. This involves recognizing and affirming one's capabilities and judgments, which can often feel compromised by the uncertainties accompanying anxious attachment patterns.

To build self-trust, start by acknowledging your emotions and instincts as valid. Rather than dismissing your feelings as irrational or unfounded, permit yourself to explore and understand them. Keep a journal to document your thoughts and emotional responses. This practice allows you to reflect on your experiences, validate your feelings, and track your growth over time. By seeing your emotions in writing, you may also realize patterns in your thinking that you can address more effectively.

Another crucial step is setting realistic expectations for yourself. Understand that recovery is not a destination but a journey. This understanding will help you be patient and kind to yourself, allowing you to make mistakes and learn from them. Celebrating your small victories is essential, as these moments build a reservoir of trust in your capabilities.

Self-care is also integral to building trust. Engaging in activities improves your physical, emotional, and mental well-being. These can be anything from exercise and meditation to pursuing hobbies you love. When you prioritize your needs, you tell yourself you are worthy of attention and care, further strengthening your self-trust.

Finally, practice positive self-talk. Challenge negative internal dialogues that undermine your confidence by identifying them when they occur and consciously replacing them with positive affirmations. Focus on your strengths and past successes instead of what could go wrong or what you fear. Positive affirmations can be powerful tools to reshape your self-perception and reinforce your belief in your abilities.

By consciously cultivating self-trust through these practices, you mitigate the effects of anxious attachment and empower yourself to engage more deeply and authentically in your relationships. It is a gradual process, but each step you take toward trusting yourself lays the groundwork for healthier connections with others, giving you a sense of control and confidence.

CHAPTER 4
INNER CHILD HEALING

IMAGINE YOURSELF AS A FIVE-YEAR-OLD CHILD, AND THERE IS A SCARY thunderstorm outside, and you are clutching a beloved stuffed animal for comfort. You feel small, scared, and craving reassurance. Now, imagine that this child exists within you, carrying the emotional weight of traumatic childhood experiences into your adult life. This is the essence of the inner child—the part of you that holds your childhood memories, emotions, and unmet needs.

INTRODUCTION TO INNER CHILD WORK

The concept of the inner child is a powerful representation of one's childhood self. It encompasses the feelings, memories, and experiences from your early years that continue to influence your adult behaviors and emotions. Much more than just a metaphor, your inner child is a fundamental part of your psyche that holds the emotional imprints of your formative years. These emotional memories can be both positive and negative, shaping how you interact with the world around you. During adulthood, when your inner child feels scared or unheard, its old wounds can resurface. This can impact your relationships and sense of self-worth.

If you have an anxious attachment, you need to address your inner child. Your insecurities and fears as an adult are often rooted in unresolved childhood traumas. When you work on reconnecting with your inner child, you will start to comprehend and heal childhood wounds. In this process, you recognize that you have had unmet needs and pain in the past, which lets you address them and show self-compassion. Healing your inner child means creating a more stable and loving inner world, which can transform your relationships today.

The inner child concept has its roots in Gestalt therapy and other therapeutic approaches in psychology. In Gestalt therapy, we see an emphasis on how our past experiences impact our present self. Inner child work became popular in the 1980s when John Bradshaw, an expert in the field, discussed it. In Bradshaw's work, there was a focus on the ways that childhood abuse, neglect, and abandonment manifest in adult behaviors, including addiction and codependency. He believed healing these childhood wounds was essential for personal growth and emotional well-being.

John Bradshaw emphasized how unresolved childhood traumas can lead to adult problems. He did research and held workshops that assisted many people in confronting their past and beginning the healing process. To address these deep-rooted issues, his approach combines different therapeutic approaches, including CBT and DBT (dialectical behavior therapy). His work has inspired many therapists to make inner child healing part of their practice, recognizing its importance in addressing the root causes of emotional distress.

Many people misunderstand inner child work. One of the most common misconceptions is that it is only for those with severe trauma. However, everyone has an inner child, and everyone can benefit from this healing process. Whether your childhood experiences were mildly unsettling or deeply traumatic, you can get profound insights and emotional healing from reconnecting with your inner child. You might also believe inner child work is too painful or difficult to engage with. While it can be challenging, the rewards far outweigh the discomfort. Confronting and healing your past can lead to profound personal growth and healthier relationships.

Another misconception is that inner child work is not scientifically supported. However, many studies and therapeutic practices validate its effectiveness. Research in psychology and neuroscience shows that early experiences shape our brain development and emotional responses. Addressing these foundational experiences can rewire your brain and create new, healthier behavior patterns. Techniques such as visualization, journaling, and therapeutic dialogue with the inner child are grounded in evidence-based practices and have demonstrated effective emotional healing.

When you do inner child work, you embark on self-discovery and healing. It is time to understand the concept of the inner child and its significance so you can begin to address unresolved traumas, reconnect with lost parts of yourself, and build a foundation for emotional security.

CONNECTING WITH YOUR INNER CHILD

Several techniques help you establish a connection with your inner child. First, creating a safe space for inner child work is essential. Start by setting up a comfortable physical space to relax and focus. For example, you could set up a cozy corner of your home with soft lighting, comfortable seating, and calming objects like candles, plants, or favorite books. Using calming and comforting objects can enhance the sense of safety. Consider including items that remind you of your childhood, such as a favorite toy or a blanket. Mindfulness is also crucial to establishing emotional safety. Practice mindfulness techniques to stay present and grounded. Deep breathing exercises, body scans, or gentle yoga can help create a calm and nurturing environment for working on your inner child.

Set intentions when you start connecting with your inner child. It is crucial to set intentions. Decide what you want to achieve from encountering your inner child, whether understanding a specific emotion, addressing an experience, or simply offering comfort. Use guided visualization as a tool for this initial meeting. Close your eyes and imagine a safe and welcoming place. This is where you should visualize and gently approach your younger self. Take note of their appearance, expressions, and emotions. Reflect on this experience and how you felt during the process. After you have finished your visualization, record your thoughts and feelings in a notebook or journal. Include what you observed and how your inner child responded. This reflection lets you better process the encounter and plan your next steps.

Visualization exercises can also be beneficial here. Imagine yourself as a child, perhaps in a place where you felt safe and happy. Picture every detail vividly—the colors, the sounds, the smells. Visualize your younger self and approach them with kindness and curiosity. Another technique is dialoguing with your inner child. This involves having a mental or written conversation with your younger self. Ask questions like, "How are you feeling?" or "What do you need?" Listen to the responses with empathy and understanding. Creative activities such as drawing or writing letters to your inner child can also be powerful. These activities allow you to tangibly express your emotions and thoughts, fostering a deeper connection.

You must do regular check-ins to create a trusting and loving relationship with your inner child. Set a daily habit of connecting with your inner child. This could be through a quick mental check-in, a short journal entry, or a brief visualization exercise. It is essential to acknowledge and validate the emotions of your inner child. When your inner child expresses fear, sadness, or joy, accept these emotions without judgment. Tell your inner child that you recognize their feelings, acknowledging their validity. Showing love and compassion toward your inner child can take many forms. Speak kindly to your inner child, offer words of comfort, and reassure them that they are loved and safe. This ongoing nurturing helps build a strong and secure relationship, allowing your inner child to heal and thrive.

IDENTIFYING CHILDHOOD TRAUMAS

Identifying childhood traumas is a crucial step in the healing process. Reflecting on significant childhood events can help you pinpoint moments that left a lasting impact. However, it is best to have support systems when you are trying to heal childhood traumas. Seeking professional help from therapists can provide the structured support you may need. Therapists trained in trauma-informed care can guide you through the healing process with empathy and expertise.

You could also benefit from joining support groups. These groups offer a sense of community and understanding, allowing you to share your experiences and learn from others facing similar challenges. It is helpful if you can lean on trusted friends and family. You may get emotional support and validation by sharing your journey with loved ones. If they give you support, it can help you feel less isolated and more connected.

To begin with, think about times when you felt scared, lonely, or unsupported. These could be moments when you were bullied at school, felt neglected by a caregiver, or experienced a family breakup. It is also crucial to recognize signs of unresolved trauma. Potential symptoms include recurring nightmares, intense emotional reactions to specific triggers, and persistent feelings of insecurity. An excellent way to further explore these memories is to write journaling prompts, such as "What is my earliest memory of feeling afraid or alone?" or "What events from my childhood still affect me today?" You will find that writing about these experiences can help you achieve clarity and understand their influence on how you currently feel and behave.

Specific therapeutic approaches can help you in healing childhood traumas. EMDR is one of these methods. In this therapy, you recall distressing memories while engaging in bilateral stimulation, such as moving your eyes from side to side or tapping. This process helps you reframe traumatic memories so that they become less overwhelming. Somatic experiencing focuses on the body's physical responses to trauma. It lets you use gentle movements and awareness of bodily sensations to help you release stored tension and trauma. Cognitive-behavioral techniques are also effective. They involve identifying and challenging negative thought patterns that stem from childhood experiences, replacing them with healthier, more balanced perspectives.

You can make these strategies part of your life to help you identify childhood traumas and foster healing and a sense of self-compassion and emotional security. Build a support system by seeking professional help, joining support groups, and leaning on trusted friends and family. Reflect on significant childhood events, recognize signs of unresolved trauma, and use journaling to explore your memories. Look into therapeutic approaches like EMDR, somatic experiencing, and cognitive-behavioral techniques and how these techniques may help you. Following these steps gives you the best chance to work toward healing and creating a healthier, more fulfilling life.

EXERCISES FOR INNER CHILD HEALING

Creative expression is often a powerful way to heal your inner child. For example, you could try drawing or painting childhood memories. It lets you visually explore and process past experiences. You do not need to be an artist to benefit from this exercise. Simply sketching scenes from your childhood can bring buried emotions to the surface. Consider creating a collage of images representing your childhood using magazines, photos, and other materials. This artistic process helps reconnect you with your younger self so you can understand the emotions tied to those memories.

Try writing letters to your inner child. Start by addressing your younger self and acknowledging their feelings and experiences. Write as if you are speaking to a dear friend, providing comfort and understanding. You might begin with, "Dear [Your Name], I remember how you felt when..." With this exercise, you validate your inner child's emotions and provide the reassurance they needed back then. Creating a scrapbook of positive childhood experiences can also be a healing practice. Gather photos and mementos, and write down happy memories. This scrapbook serves as a reminder of the joy and love you experienced, helping to balance the painful memories.

You can also find guided meditations that connect you with your inner child and provide comfort. These meditations often begin with a relaxation phase, helping you to calm your mind and body. A meditation script might guide you to visualize a safe, peaceful place where you can meet your inner child. Imagine holding their hand, offering words of reassurance, and listening to their concerns. Many people find it soothing to visualize comforting and nurturing your inner child. Picture yourself wrapping them in a warm blanket or reading them a bedtime story. Audio resources for guided meditations are widely available and valuable in your healing practice.

Role-playing scenarios can be another effective way to re-enact and heal past experiences. Make sure that you have a trusted partner for these kinds of exercises. They let you revisit specific events from your childhood in a safe and supportive environment. For example, you might role-play a conversation with a parent or teacher, expressing feelings you could not articulate at the time. You could also try therapeutic role-playing in a group setting. This might allow you to share your experiences with others with similar traumas, providing a sense of solidarity and understanding. Using role-playing to practice new responses to old triggers can help you develop healthier coping mechanisms. You get to rehearse new behaviors, making it easier for you to integrate them into your daily life, reducing the impact of past traumas.

Daily affirmations are yet another powerful tool for reinforcing inner child healing. Writing personalized affirmations that address your inner child's needs and fears can be healing. Does your inner child feel unworthy? You could use the affirmation, "I deserve love and respect." When you incorporate the right affirmations into your daily routine, they can help solidify new positive beliefs. Repeat them in the morning, before bed, or during moments of stress. Over the long term, your daily affirmations can be a transformational tool for healing. Keep a journal to note changes in your feelings and behaviors, celebrating the small victories.

Ultimately, you must practice self-compassion and forgiveness for a successful healing process. Self-compassion exercises can help you treat yourself with the kindness and understanding you would offer a friend. For example, when you notice self-critical thoughts, use compassionate language in reframing.

Another powerful tool is guided meditation for self-forgiveness. These meditations guide you through visualizing forgiveness, helping you release guilt and shame associated with past events. Writing forgiveness letters to yourself is another effective technique. In these letters, acknowledge the pain you have experienced and give yourself forgiveness and understanding. This act of self-compassion can be incredibly liberating and healing.

By making inner child exercises part of your life, you can connect profoundly with your inner child and begin to heal. Whether through creative expression, writing, guided meditations, role-playing, daily affirmations, or self-compassion, each activity offers a unique way to address and heal past wounds. These exercises will help nurture your inner child, creating a more secure and loving inner world and positively impacting your relationships and overall well-being.

HOW TO INTEGRATE INNER CHILD WORK INTO YOUR LIFE

I find doing daily inner child practices grounding and transformative. Begin each morning with a simple check-in. When you wake up each morning, close your eyes briefly and visualize your inner child. Ask them how they are feeling and what they need today. This brief mental connection sets a nurturing tone for your day. Also, before you go to bed every night, reflect on your day and your inner child's emotions at different points. If they need reassurance, provide it. These practices can help you maintain a solid emotional connection with your inner child.

Mindfulness is crucial for integrating inner child work into your daily life. With simple mindfulness practices, staying present and maintaining the proper emotional connection is much easier. I recommend doing mindful breathing exercises, as they can center you in the present moment. Take a few minutes to focus on your breath, inhaling deeply and exhaling slowly. This practice calms your mind, allowing you to tune into your inner child's emotions. Practicing presence in everyday activities can also help you. Try to be mindful in daily activities, such as eating, walking, and working. Notice the sights, sounds, and sensations around you. This mindfulness is critical to staying grounded and aware of your inner child's needs and emotions.

Daily rituals can also honor the presence of your inner child. These rituals do not have to be elaborate. Simple acts like enjoying a favorite childhood snack, listening to music that brings back happy memories, or spending time on a beloved hobby can be meaningful. These activities are helpful reminders for nurturing and caring for your inner child, integrating their needs into your daily life. You can gain much insight by journaling your interactions with your inner child. Document these moments to track your progress and understand the evolving relationship with your inner self.

Maintain a balance between your inner child's needs and your adult responsibilities. You achieve this through thoughtful boundary-setting. Set times for your inner child work, ensuring it does not interfere with your daily tasks. For instance, you might set aside fifteen minutes in the morning and evening for this practice. Prioritizing self-care without neglecting your responsibilities is critical. Ensure you meet your basic needs, such as proper nutrition, sleep, and exercise. Taking care of yourself is one way to care for your inner child. Creating a harmonious relationship between your inner child and adult self involves recognizing that both aspects of you need attention. Allow your inner child to influence your choices in ways that bring joy and creativity while your adult self manages responsibilities and decision-making.

Tracking my progress and reflecting on my inner child healing journey is immensely helpful for growth. Keep a progress journal to document your experiences, emotions, and insights. Reflective questions can guide your journaling, helping you assess your growth. Ask yourself, "How have my interactions with my inner child changed over time?" or "What new insights have I gained about my childhood experiences?" Answering questions like these means you do deep reflection and achieve better self-awareness. Remember to celebrate your milestones and achievements. Acknowledge small victories, like comforting your inner child during a moment of distress or gaining a new understanding of an experience. These celebrations reinforce your progress and motivate you to continue doing the necessary work to heal.

Case Studies in Inner Child Healing

In my journey, I have found looking at success stories to be a great source of inspiration. So, let's take a look at Emily's journey. Emily had always struggled with intense fear of abandonment, stemming from her parents' tumultuous divorce when she was just seven. She felt responsible for the split and carried this guilt into her adult relationships, always craving validation. Through inner child work, Emily began visualizing herself as that scared little girl, offering comfort and reassurance. She wrote letters to her younger self, expressing the love and support she had longed for. Over time, Emily's fear transformed into confidence, and she learned to trust herself and her relationships.

James's story is another powerful example. Growing up, James experienced frequent criticism from his father, leaving him deep-seated feelings of inadequacy. The result was struggling with self-compassion as an adult. He frequently criticized himself for even the most minor mistakes. Fortunately, James started to do guided meditations and self-compassion exercises, and in doing so, he began to reconnect with his inner child. He visualized holding his younger self, offering words of kindness and understanding. This practice helped James develop a sense of self-worth and self-love. He learned to practice self-forgiveness for past mistakes and embrace his imperfections. James's path to self-compassion transformed his relationships, making them more authentic and fulfilling.

Reflect on these stories and consider how they may resonate with your experiences. Ask yourself, "What childhood events have shaped my current behaviors?" or "How can I offer my inner child the support they need?" These reflective questions can help you see similarities between your journey and those of Emily and James. This can give you more insight into the whole process and how to proceed. Remember that you are never alone as you navigate your inner child healing journey. Countless other people have walked this path and achieved healing and transformation.

REPARENTING YOURSELF: STEPS AND STRATEGIES

The whole process of healing your inner child can be summed up around "reparenting yourself." It is a transformative approach to healing anxious attachment and fostering healthier relationships. This process involves nurturing and caring for your inner child—the part of you that may feel neglected, anxious, or unworthy due to past experiences. By actively reparenting, you can develop a secure attachment style, rebuild trust, and cultivate lasting love.

Steps to Reparent Yourself:

1. **Understand Your Inner Child**: To begin your reparenting journey, you must recognize and understand your inner child. This part of you carries the emotional imprints of joyful and painful childhood experiences. Anxious attachment often stems from unmet needs during our formative years, such as a lack of emotional support or inconsistent caregiving. By acknowledging the presence of your inner child, you can start to address the fears and insecurities that arise in adult relationships.

2. **Be Aware of and Acknowledge Emotions**: Begin by understanding your feelings and behaviors related to anxious attachment. Journaling can be an effective tool here. Write about moments when you feel uneasy in relationships and explore the triggers behind these feelings. Acknowledge your inner child's emotions and needs without judgment.

3. **Create a Safe Space**: Establish a mental or physical environment that feels safe and nurturing. It could be a cozy corner in your home or a visualization of a comforting place. When you feel anxious, retreat to this space, inviting your inner child to join you. Use this safe space to reflect, breathe, and ground yourself. Guided visualizations, where we create a safe space for their inner child, can offer comfort and reassurance.

4. **Engage in Dialogue**: Interacting with your inner child through dialogue is a powerful tool for reparenting. Set aside time to write letters to your inner child, expressing love and reassurance. You can also ask your inner child questions—encouraging them to share their fears and desires. Respond to their needs with compassion and understanding, reinforcing a sense of security. Additionally, rewriting personal narratives to reframe past experiences can help transform how we perceive ourselves and our relationships. These healing steps can significantly reduce the impact of adverse childhood experiences on attachment styles, offering a hopeful path for the future.

5. **Nurture Your Needs**: Identify and meet your emotional and physical needs as a caring parent would, including setting boundaries, prioritizing self-care, and engaging in activities that bring you joy and fulfillment. You might also explore mindfulness practices to stay present and calm during anxiety-provoking moments.

6. **Practice Self-Compassion**: Treat yourself with the kindness and empathy you would offer a frightened child. When you encounter feelings of anxiety, remind yourself

that it is okay to feel this way. Use affirmations to foster self-acceptance: "I am worthy of love" or "It is safe for me to open my heart." Regularly reaffirming your values and needs helps build a more supportive inner dialogue.

7. **Seek Support**: Reparenting can be challenging, and you may benefit from additional support. Consider working with a therapist specializing in attachment theory to guide you through this process. A therapist can help us explore how past experiences shape our current behaviors and relationships. They can provide valuable tools and perspectives to help you navigate your journey toward healing wounds. This process of gaining awareness and processing painful memories in a safe environment can lead to healthier attachment patterns.

8. **Reflect on Your Healing Journey**: Personal reflection is essential for growth. Think about keeping a reflection journal where you document your experiences, insights, and emotions. You can write on questions such as "What progress have I made in connecting with my inner child?" or "How have my relationships changed due to this work?" Additionally, you can share your reflections in support groups. Doing this can provide additional perspectives and encouragement. The community aspect of healing is vital. Sharing your experiences creates a space for mutual understanding and support, fostering a sense of belonging and solidarity.

Cultivating Lasting Self-Love

As you engage in reparenting, you are healing the wounds of your past and setting the foundation for more secure and fulfilling relationships. By addressing your anxious attachment, you can cultivate a deep sense of self-love, which ultimately paves the way for nurturing connections with others. Taking these healing steps can significantly reduce the impact of adverse childhood experiences on attachment styles.

Finally, reparenting yourself is an ongoing process that requires patience and dedication. The more you understand and care for your inner child, the more you will reclaim your sense of worth and the ability to love and be loved without fear. The journey may be challenging, but the growth and healing that await will empower you to build the solid and lasting relationships you genuinely deserve.

CHAPTER 5
BUILDING TRUST AND EMOTIONAL SECURITY IN YOUR RELATIONSHIPS

IMAGINE HOW YOU WOULD FEEL STANDING NEAR THE EDGE OF A CLIFF, looking down at the vast, unknown expanse below. Your heart races, your palms sweat, and you feel overwhelmed by the fear of falling. You might have this emotion when trust is broken in a relationship, and it illustrates how deeper trust is essential for building better emotional security and ensuring healthy and long-lasting relationships.

UNDERSTANDING AND REBUILDING TRUST

Our first step is understanding the full importance of trust—the foundation of emotional security. It is crucial for keeping relationships together. With the right level of trust, you have a feeling of safety and being valued and understood. You will be able to share your deepest fears and dreams without being afraid of judgment or betrayal. Building better trust also profoundly improves relationship satisfaction. You will enjoy more open communication and a stronger feeling of partnership and mutual respect. When you lack trust, your relationship can become unstable and filled with doubt and insecurity. Successful relationships, whether romantic, familial, or platonic, have a solid foundation of trust. When you look at couples who have weathered storms together, their bond has often become more robust because they trust each other's intentions and actions.

Make sure that you identify any trust issues in your relationship. There are different signs of broken trust you should look out for. For example, do you frequently desire to check your partner's phone, question their whereabouts, or doubt what they say? This kind of behavior indicates that there are probably underlying trust issues. You can also do reflective exercises to help you pinpoint these issues. Take the time to think about the root reasons for feelings of distrust. Did one specific incident shatter your trust? Or has there been a gradual buildup of distrust because you have been constantly let down?

It is best to take a structured approach to rebuilding trust. You first need to acknowledge the breach of trust and take steps to address it. For the problem to be resolved, both partners must recognize the issue and commit to making the necessary changes. It is crucial to have consistent and transparent communication. Openly share your emotions and practice active listening when considering your partner's concerns without judgment. You will find that transparency on both sides builds trust over time. Remember to demonstrate your reliability and dependability. Stay faithful to your promises, showing that you follow through. This includes even promises that seem small or relatively insignificant. If you say you will be home by seven, ensure you are. By taking this action course, you demonstrate to your partner that they can count on you. This will eventually help them rebuild their trust in you.

Be persistent in monitoring how you progress in rebuilding the trust in your relationship. I have found it helpful to keep a trust journal. That is where you will write down your thoughts and feelings and any significant interactions related to trust. By doing this, you will find it easier to keep track of how you progress and notice areas in need of improvement. You should set short-term and long-term goals. Examples of short-term goals can be daily acts of transparency, such as sharing your schedule. A long-term goal is rebuilding emotional intimacy. It is essential to check in regularly with your partner. Set aside time each week to talk about your progress and feelings and make the adjustments you find you need to make. With these conversations, you can help foster a stronger sense of partnership and mutual commitment to rebuilding trust.

You can get valuable insights from contemplating the steps you have taken and how much progress you have made. In this process, you might see that while some actions have helped you make great strides in rebuilding trust, others have not been as successful. Remember that the path toward rebuilding trust is not linear. There will be setbacks, but each step forward strengthens your relationship's foundation.

COMMUNICATION TECHNIQUES FOR TRUST-BUILDING

Trust-building is impossible without effective communication. Good communication can create a foundation of understanding and respect, which is essential to any healthy relationship. Active listening is a crucial part of that. With active listening, you focus entirely on what your partner is saying, ensuring you understand what they are communicating. Ensure you do not interrupt, and show engagement by nodding and with verbal cues, such as "I understand" or "Tell me more." Active listening shows your partner you value their feelings and perspective, creating a safe space for meaningful conversations. Open and honest dialogue is another vital principle. Seek transparency about how you feel and what you think, which will help foster trust. Non-verbal communication cues also play a significant role. Your body language, facial expressions, and tone of voice can communicate more than words. Be mindful of your non-verbal cues and be attentive to your partner's. Ensure that your non-verbal cues are aligned with your verbal messages when demonstrating engagement and concern.

You will find specific techniques helpful in maintaining transparency in communication. The "I" statement technique is particularly effective. You express your feelings and needs by starting sentences with "I," so you do not give the impression of placing blame. Here is an example. Instead of saying, "You never listen to me," you could say, "I feel unheard when we do not discuss things openly." By using this approach, you cut down on the chance of defensiveness, creating the conditions for a more open dialogue. It is an excellent idea to do reflective listening exercises to help maintain transparency. After your partner speaks, tell them what you heard and how you interpreted their statement to ensure you understood their intended meaning. For instance, say, "What I hear you saying is that you feel neglected when I work late." When you do this kind of active listening, you validate your partner's feelings and clarify any potential misunderstandings. You should also do regular relationship check-ins. Set aside time each week to discuss your relationship, share your feelings, and address any concerns. You create regular, open, honest communication opportunities by doing check-ins like these, reinforcing trust over time.

Seek to resolve your conflicts in a way that builds trust and requires you to remain calm and composed. Avoid engaging when emotions are high; when people do, they tend to say things they do not mean, and the situation can escalate. Breathe deeply and keep your focus on staying calm. You can also try collaborative problem-solving techniques. Adopt the spirit of teamwork in how you approach conflict, working to find solutions that satisfy both partners. For example, you could brainstorm ideas, weigh pros and cons, compromise, and negotiate. Compromise and negotiation are crucial in this process. Recognize that you might not get everything you want, but finding a middle ground can strengthen your relationship. Just say you and your partner disagree on how you want to spend a weekend. Try finding a way to incorporate both of your preferences. By adopting this collaborative approach, you foster mutual respect and trust.

You need strong communication to build emotional intimacy, which has a strong link with trust. You can deepen your connection by sharing personal stories and vulnerabilities. You invite your partner to do the same when you open up about your fears, dreams, and past experiences. This creates a mutual vulnerability that fosters trust and emotional closeness. Another way to improve emotional intimacy is by expressing appreciation and gratitude. Regularly tell your partner what you appreciate about them and your relationship. This positive reinforcement fosters a stronger bond and makes your partner feel valued. Engaging in meaningful conversations is equally essential. Talk about topics that matter to you both. Examples might be your personal goals and shared interests. These conversations foster a deeper understanding of each other, strengthening your emotional connection.

Practicing these communication techniques allows you to gradually rebuild and strengthen the trust between you and your partner. You will have to be patient and consistent with this process. Through this process, you can create a relationship in which trust and emotional security flourish.

CREATING A SECURE BASE: FOUNDATIONS OF EMOTIONAL SECURITY

For any relationship to have emotional security, it needs a secure base. Picture a child venturing out to explore a playground, constantly looking back to ensure their caregiver is there so that they can feel safe. As I discussed earlier, this concept from attachment theory extends to our relationships in adulthood. With a secure base, you feel stability and reassurance, letting you explore the world and take emotional risks, knowing you have a dependable safety net. This plays a vital role in fostering emotional security. A secure base means that you can feel confident to express your true self, knowing your partner will be there to support you. A few examples of secure base behaviors include frequent check-ins, comfort during stressful times, and showing that you are a reliable presence in daily life.

Specific characteristics are necessary for a secure base in a relationship. Two of these are consistency and reliability. Predictability in your partner's actions and responses is critical to building trust. You can feel secure knowing they will be there when you need them. It is also crucial to have emotional availability and support. You must be emotionally and physically present when your partner needs you. You must engage in active listening, validate emotions, and provide comfort. Mutual respect and achieving a better understanding further strengthen a secure base. This means acknowledging each other's needs, boundaries, and perspectives. Also, you and your partner should appreciate the unique qualities each of you brings to the relationship.

You need to use intentional actions and practices in building a secure base. Create rituals of connection, as they can be a powerful way to strengthen your bond. Examples of these rituals might be daily check-ins and weekly date nights. They could even be simple acts, such as enjoying coffee together each morning. With these shared moments, you foster a feeling of togetherness and dependability. Another essential step is making sure that you are emotionally available. Being there for your partner is a top priority, especially when they are going through challenging times.

In many cases, this might involve setting distractions aside so that you can fully listen and provide a comforting presence when they feel stressed. It is also crucial to practice supportive behaviors consistently. This involves demonstrating empathy, offering help without your partner having to ask, and celebrating the successes each of you achieves.

You can do specific reflective exercises to assess and strengthen your secure base. Begin with ones that help you evaluate the current state of your relationship. Ask yourself questions such as, "Do I feel safe and supported by my partner?" or "Are there areas where I feel more vulnerable?" The next thing to do is identify areas where your relationship can improve. Maybe you realize that while your partner makes you feel emotionally supported, you see that daily interactions lack some consistency. Put changes into motion by setting specific goals.

An example might be agreeing to have a daily debrief. This is a time when each of you shares your highs and lows of the day. Remember to keep track of your progress. I like keeping a journal documenting how these changes impact your sense of security. You can think about what you notice there and discuss your observations with your partner regularly.

Strengthening a secure base is an ongoing process. You and your partner must show commitment to maintaining and improving the relationship. You will strengthen your relationship by regularly revisiting and assessing your efforts, ensuring both partners feel secure and valued. Focusing on these practices will help you build a resilient and supportive foundation that improves your connection and emotional security.

OVERCOMING MISTRUST: STRATEGIES AND EXERCISES

You need to understand the origin of your mistrust before you can effectively address it in your relationship. In many cases, past experiences and traumas lead to mistrust. Being betrayed in any relationship can leave deep scars. When you have scars like these, you will find it difficult to trust someone again fully. That is because you are constantly on guard, waiting for history to repeat itself. Your trust is eroded by someone who breaks promises and behaves inconsistently.

When someone says one thing but does another, it creates confusion and doubt. Over time, these inconsistencies can accumulate, and this can cause you to question whether the person you are dealing with is genuinely reliable. Other factors that can have an impact include external influences and pressures. Our views on trust and trustworthiness are affected by societal expectations, peer pressure, and cultural norms. Did you grow up in an environment that was full of mistrust? If so, you will likely find it challenging to free yourself from that way of thinking.

Fortunately, there are cognitive techniques that can help you challenge and change your mistrustful thoughts. Begin by noticing your negative thought patterns. Do you find that you always tend to assume the worst? Take a moment to recognize this pattern. Once you have identified a pattern like this, challenge these negative thoughts by asking yourself for evidence. If you keep imagining that your partner is untrustworthy, ask yourself if these fears are based on past experiences. Are there any objective reasons you should feel mistrustful? If not, challenge your thoughts and reframe them. With reframing, instead of thinking, "They are probably lying to me," try to reframe it to, "I have no reason to doubt their honesty right now." This will help you develop more balance in how you perceive and think about things. You will find it easier to see situations from a neutral standpoint. With this perspective, you can recognize that while there may be risks in trusting someone, you also get life-enhancing opportunities for deep, meaningful connections.

You should also consider using behavioral strategies to build trust. A great example of this is showing your reliability with your actions. Remember, actions speak louder than words. Ensure you follow through if you have said you will do something. When you show consistency in your actions, it helps build a stronger foundation of trust. You can also take part in trust-building activities. Examples of these activities include spending quality time together, working on joint projects, or simply being there for each other during tough times. When you consistently follow through on commitments, no matter how small, that reinforces trust. That is because it demonstrates that you are dependable and that your words match your actions.

You may find specific exercises helpful to overcome mistrust for couples. An excellent place to start is with trust-building conversations. Set aside time to discuss your fears and concerns openly. Use "I" statements to express how specific actions make you feel without placing blame. Joint goal-setting activities can also create more trust. Working together toward a common goal, whether planning a trip or saving for a house, fosters a sense of partnership and mutual reliance. It is also helpful to practice forgiveness and letting go. Holding onto past grievances only fuels mistrust. Learn to forgive and move forward, shifting your focus to building a positive future together.

Reflective exercises can help you and your partner work through mistrust. An example could be writing down three instances where you felt mistrustful and then discussing them together. Identify what triggered these emotions and tactics for addressing them moving forward. You can also integrate trust-building activities into your daily routine. Strengthen your bond with simple acts like sharing a distraction-free meal or relaxing and discussing your day. To practice forgiveness, you must recognize past hurts and consciously decide to let them go. This does not mean forgetting what happened. It just means choosing not to allow past pain to dictate your current relationship.

Both partners must commit to overcoming mistrust to improve the relationship. Focus on building new, positive experiences that counteract past hurts. As we have seen here, we can create a stronger, more resilient relationship when we understand the origins of mistrust, use cognitive and behavioral strategies, and participate in trust-building exercises. Be patient. Trust is never rebuilt overnight. Instead, it takes commitment and dedication.

TRUST-BUILDING ACTIVITIES FOR COUPLES

Doing joint activities is a highly effective way of building better trust in relationships. That is because shared experiences create a bond that cannot be achieved with words alone. When you engage in activities together, you can show dependability and consistency. This is especially true in settings that require teamwork and mutual support. For example, going on a challenging hike together brings you closer physically and emotionally. You build a sense of partnership and mutual reliance as you navigate the trail together. Completing such activities strengthens the emotional connection, reinforcing that you can depend on each other in various situations.

There are many types of joint activities, each with its unique way of building trust. Try adventure-based activities if you want something requiring you to depend on each other and bond more closely. Examples are hiking and team sports. For instance, navigating a problematic trail together or competing in a friendly game fosters a sense of teamwork and partnership. Another great choice of trust-building activity is a collaborative project, such as a home improvement task or trip planning. These projects require you and your partner to develop better coordination, communication, and shared responsibility—all critical components of trust. Intimacy-building activities like couple's yoga or dance classes offer another layer. These activities require you to be present and connected, both physically and emotionally. In this way, they enhance your bond and trust.

There are specific guidelines to remember when planning and doing trust-building activities. First, ensuring that you and your partner are interested in the activity and fully willing to participate is vital. Do not pressure your partner to participate in something they do not want. When both are interested in an activity, you have an equal chance of enjoying yourself and getting meaning from the experience. Next, set clear expectations and goals. Before you start the activity, talk about what you hope to achieve and any boundaries or limitations. Clear communication from the outset helps to prevent misunderstandings and ensures that both partners are on the same page. You should also reflect on the experiences you had during the activity afterward. Discuss what you enjoyed, what you found challenging, and how the activity affected your relationship. This reflection will help solidify the activity's positive effects and reinforce trust.

Let's take a look at Mark and Lisa. They decided to take up adventure sports to build trust and reconnect. Their first activity was rock climbing, something neither had done before. The experience required them to rely on each other for safety and encouragement. They faced challenges and fears initially but gave each other the needed support. They felt renewed trust and partnership when the climb was finished. I recommend thinking about some reflective questions after an experience like this. You could ask yourself questions such as, "How did this activity make me feel about my partner?" or "What did I learn about our ability to work together?" These questions encourage you to reflect deeply to understand how the activity impacts your relationship.

Many trust-building activities are available, and you can tailor them to resonate with you and your partner. The key is to engage in activities that require cooperation, communication, and mutual support. Whether it is adventure sports, collaborative projects, or intimacy-building exercises, these activities offer a hands-on way to strengthen your bond and build trust. By following the guidelines of mutual interest, clear expectations, and post-activity reflection, you can maximize the benefits of these experiences. Over time, these shared moments will create a stronger, more resilient foundation of trust in your relationship.

HOW TO HANDLE SETBACKS IN TRUST-BUILDING

You should know how to recognize common setbacks in the trust-building process. Relationships are complex, and setbacks are inevitable. For example, you might occasionally relapse into old behaviors, such as feeling unreasonably suspicious and overreacting to minor issues. You will feel frustrated, but it is all part of the process. You should also be prepared for potential miscommunications and misunderstandings. You might say something with one intention, but your partner interprets it differently. These misunderstandings can lead to unnecessary conflicts and feelings of distrust. External stressors, such as work pressure, financial strain, or family issues, can also impact your relationship. When stressed, we are more likely to misinterpret what our partners say, which can lead to further mistrust.

You will need to have open and honest discussions when setbacks occur. When there is a setback, discuss it openly with your partner. Acknowledge the issue without placing blame. Discuss what happened, how it made you feel, and how you can avoid similar setbacks in the future. Be open to reassessing and adjusting your trust-building plans. Do not be fearful about changing your strategy if it is not working. Flexibility is key. You should try different approaches to find what works best for you both. Seeking external support can also be beneficial. Sometimes, an outside perspective can provide valuable insights. For example, you could talk to a therapist or counselor specializing in relationships. They can offer guidance and strategies to help you navigate setbacks.

You need to maintain resilience and commitment in the trust-building process. Recognize the importance of maintaining your motivation even when challenges try to hold you back. Remind yourself why you are putting in the effort, and keep focusing on the positive changes you have already made. Be patient, and realize that trust is not rebuilt overnight. It takes time, and there will be ups and downs. Celebrate small victories and progress. No matter how small, each step forward is a sign of growth. Recognize and appreciate these moments. They can provide the motivation you need to keep going.

You have an opportunity for growth when you learn from setbacks. Reflect on what caused them, asking yourself what triggered the issue and how you responded. This reflection can help you understand the underlying patterns and behaviors that led to the setback. The next thing to do is identify the lessons you have learned. Think about what you could have done differently and what strategies might be more effective in the future. Implementing changes to prevent future setbacks is crucial. Make adjustments to your approach by contemplating the insights you gained during reflection. For example, if you realize that external stressors often lead to misunderstandings, find ways to manage stress more effectively. This proactive approach can help you avoid similar issues in the future.

You can navigate the trust-building process optimally by recognizing common setbacks, addressing them openly, maintaining resilience, and learning from each experience. Remember, setbacks are not failures. Instead, they are opportunities to learn and grow. Embrace them as part of your journey toward building a stronger, more trusting relationship.

CHAPTER 6
STRENGTHENING RELATIONSHIP SKILLS

COMMUNICATION STRATEGIES AND EXERCISES

THINK ABOUT A TIME WHEN YOU FELT UNHEARD IN A CONVERSATION. Maybe your words were bouncing off a brick wall of indifference. The frustration and isolation that followed stayed with you, making you wary of speaking up again. This experience is all too common, reminding us that communication is essential in relationships. Communication is the lifeblood of any relationship, and mastering it can transform your connections, turning misunderstandings into clarity and conflict into cooperation.

Active Listening Techniques

Imagine a conversation where you feel honestly heard and understood. The person you speak with is fully present, reflecting on your words and asking clarifying questions. This is the essence of active listening, a skill that can transform relationships by fostering understanding and trust. Active listening goes beyond merely hearing words; it involves engaging with the speaker on a deeper level. While passive listening might involve nodding without truly processing the message, active listening requires full attention and participation. This difference is crucial. Active listening can change the dynamics of a relationship, making interactions more meaningful and reducing misunderstandings.

One of the core components of active listening is paying full attention to the speaker. This means setting aside distractions, maintaining eye contact, and being present in the moment. When you give someone your undivided attention, you value their words and feelings. Reflecting on what you hear is another vital aspect. This involves paraphrasing or summarizing the speaker's message to ensure you understand correctly. For instance, if your partner says, "I have been feeling overwhelmed at work," you might respond, "So, you are feeling a lot of pressure right now?" This reflection not only clarifies the message but also shows empathy and understanding.

You should also ask clarifying questions whenever necessary. These questions help you gather more information and better understand the speaker's perspective. For example, you might ask, "Can you tell me more about what has been overwhelming?" or "How can I support you during this time?" Such questions demonstrate your engagement and genuine interest in the other person's experience. They also encourage the speaker to open up and share more, fostering a deeper connection.

Practicing active listening techniques can enhance your skills and improve your relationships. Paraphrasing and summarizing the speaker's message helps ensure you grasp their point. This practice can prevent misunderstandings and demonstrate that you are actively engaged in the conversation. Non-verbal cues, such as nodding, maintaining eye contact, and leaning slightly forward, can further show your engagement and interest. These cues signal to the speaker that you are fully present and invested in what they are saying.

Avoiding distractions and interruptions is crucial for active listening. Managing distractions, like putting away your phone or turning off the TV, allows you to focus entirely on the conversation. This level of attention and respect can significantly enhance the quality of your interactions. Avoid interrupting your partner, as it can disrupt the flow of their speech and make them feel unheard. Wait until they finish speaking before responding.

Active Listening Exercises for Improvement

You can do active listening exercises with a partner or friend. Choose a topic and take turns speaking and listening. After each turn, the listener should paraphrase what they heard and ask clarifying questions. Doing this exercise effectively develops your listening skills and encourages better mutual understanding. Reflective journaling on listening experiences is another valuable practice. After a conversation, take a few minutes to write about what went well and what could be improved. Reflect on your listening behaviors, such as how well you paid attention, reflected on the message, and asked clarifying questions. Use this self-reflection to gain new insight and guide your growth.

Practicing active listening in different scenarios can also enhance your skills. Try actively listening during everyday interactions, such as with colleagues at work, friends over coffee, or family members at home. Each situation offers a unique opportunity to apply and refine your listening techniques. When you consistently practice active listening, making it a natural part of your communication style is more effortless. This will lead to stronger relationships and more profound connections.

In-Depth Strategies for Effective Communication

As we saw in the previous chapter, there are certain vital principles we need to remember that are essential to effective communication. Clarity and conciseness are paramount. Aim to be clear and straightforward when expressing your thoughts and feelings. Avoid beating around the bush or using ambiguous language that can lead to misunderstandings. For instance, instead of saying, "I feel like you never listen to me," you might say, "I feel hurt when I talk, and you seem distracted." This makes your point more straightforward and reduces the likelihood of defensive reactions.

Remember the tip I provided in an earlier chapter about using "I" statements? This technique involves framing your feelings and thoughts from your perspective so that you avoid creating the impression of making accusations. For example, saying, "I feel upset when plans change without notice," is more effective than "You always change plans at the last minute." "I" statements help you take ownership of your feelings and reduce blame, fostering a more open and constructive dialogue.

Maintaining a respectful tone is equally important. Even when discussing complex subjects or expressing frustration, keep your tone calm and respectful. Avoid raising your voice, using sarcasm, or resorting to name-calling. When you communicate respectfully, you encourage your partner to listen and engage, not shut down or become defensive.

You need to know how to recognize and address defensive behaviors to overcome communication behaviors. Defense mechanisms like stonewalling, where one partner shuts down and refuses to communicate, can hinder effective communication. It is essential to address these behaviors calmly. Acknowledge the tension and suggest a break if emotions run too high. This can prevent escalation and allow for more productive discussions later.

It is essential to minimize distractions and maintain focus during conversations. Getting distracted by phones, emails, and other interruptions is too easy. Make a conscious effort to eliminate these distractions when having meaningful discussions. Put your phone on silent, turn off the TV, and find a quiet space to focus solely on the conversation. Giving your full attention to your partner shows that you value their words and are committed to understanding their perspective.

An excellent way to reduce the chance of miscommunication is to paraphrase and summarize what your partner says. This ensures that you have understood them correctly. For example, you might say, "So, what I hear you saying is that you felt ignored when I did not respond to your message. Is that correct?" This clarifies the message and shows you actively listen and engage in the conversation.

Non-verbal communication plays a significant role in how we convey and interpret messages. Reading body language and facial expressions can provide valuable context for spoken words. For instance, crossed arms and a stern expression might indicate defensiveness or discomfort, while maintaining eye contact and nodding can signal attentiveness and empathy. Understanding these cues can help you respond more appropriately and empathetically.

The tone and pitch of your voice also significantly impact how your message is received. A soft, calm tone can soothe and reassure, while a harsh or high-pitched tone can escalate tension and provoke defensive reactions. Being mindful of how you say something is just as important as what you say.

Using non-verbal cues to enhance verbal communication can strengthen your message. Simple gestures like a gentle touch on the arm, nodding in agreement, or maintaining eye contact can reinforce your words and convey sincerity and empathy. These small actions can significantly affect how your message is received and understood.

More Practice Exercises for Improving Communication Skills

Role-playing difficult conversations can be an effective way to practice and improve your communication skills. Find a trusted friend or partner and take turns role-playing various scenarios, such as discussing a sensitive issue or resolving a conflict. This practice can help you become more comfortable expressing your thoughts and feelings and develop strategies for handling challenging conversations.

Practicing active communication techniques with a partner involves setting aside time to focus solely on improving your communication. During these sessions, practice using "I" statements, maintaining a respectful tone, and employing paraphrasing and summarizing techniques. Reflect on your successes and areas for improvement, and encourage your partner to do the same. This mutual effort can enhance your communication skills and strengthen your relationship.

Reflect on your successes in communication with your partner and stay aware of areas for improvement so you can continue to grow. After a conversation, take a moment to reflect on what went well and what could be improved. Consider journaling your thoughts and feelings, noting any patterns or recurring issues. This reflection can provide valuable insights and guide you in making necessary adjustments to your communication style.

Focusing on these principles and strategies can transform your communication, fostering more profound understanding and connection in your relationships. Effective communication is a skill that you and your partner can develop and refine. With practice, it can become a powerful tool for building stronger, healthier connections.

Empathetic Responses in Relationships

Empathy is the ability to understand and share the feelings of another person. It goes beyond merely hearing words to genuinely grasping the emotions behind them. Empathy creates a bridge between people, which is essential for building deep and meaningful connections. Unlike sympathy, which often involves feeling pity for someone, empathy consists of putting yourself in their shoes and experiencing their emotions as if they were your own. In the context of a relationship, empathetic behaviors include truly listening when your partner talks about their day, comforting them when they are upset, and celebrating their successes as if they were your own. These actions demonstrate your care, helping fortify your relationship's bond.

You need to practice intentionally to develop better empathy. One strategy is called perspective-taking, and you do it by consciously trying to see a situation from another person's point of view. Imagine how they might feel and what they might be thinking. You will find it easier to respond more compassionately when you regularly do this exercise. Engaging in empathetic listening is another powerful tool. This involves entirely focusing on the speaker, reflecting on their emotions, and validating them. For example, if your partner tells you they are stressed about work, you might say, "It sounds like you are feeling overwhelmed right now. That must be tough." Another way to become more empathetic is to consider when someone shows empathy. How did it make you feel? What did they do that positively impacted you? Use these reflections to guide how you interact with others.

You can transform your relationships by expressing empathy effectively in your interactions. Verbal expressions of empathy involve acknowledging and validating the other person's feelings. Phrases like, "I can see that this hurts you" or "It sounds like you are feeling anxious" show that you are attuned to their emotional state. Non-verbal cues also play a significant role. For example, maintaining eye contact, nodding, and gentle touches can convey empathy even when you say nothing. These small gestures can make the other person feel seen and understood. Using empathetic language in challenging conversations can help de-escalate tension and foster a more constructive dialogue. Instead of saying, "You are always so negative," you might say, "I have noticed you have been feeling down lately. Can you tell me more about what's going on?" This approach shows concern and invites openness rather than defensiveness.

Empathy-Building Exercises

You can build better empathy skills by role-playing empathetic responses. Find a partner and share a recent experience while the other practices empathetic listening and responding. This exercise can help you become more comfortable expressing empathy and understanding how it feels to be on the receiving end. Another way to practice this is by doing community service or volunteer work. Helping others in need helps many people broaden their perspective and deepen their understanding of different life experiences. Make sure that you sometimes reflect on empathetic interactions and their impact. When you have conversations in which you practice empathy, take some time to journal about how it went. What did you say or do that felt empathetic? How did the other person respond? This reflection can help you identify what works well and areas for improvement.

Empathy is a powerful tool that can transform your relationships. By understanding empathy, developing it through practice, and expressing it effectively, you can create more profound, meaningful connections with the people around you. In addition to being beneficial in romantic relationships, they also enhance every other kind of connection and interaction. This includes your relationships with family, friends, colleagues, and acquaintances. Empathy means that you can understand and share the feelings of others, which fosters a sense of connection and community. Your relationships will be more resilient and emotionally fulfilling.

SETTING AND MAINTAINING HEALTHY BOUNDARIES

Understanding boundaries is crucial for fostering healthy relationships. Boundaries are like invisible lines defining where you end and others begin, ensuring your needs and limits are respected. There are various types of boundaries, including physical, emotional, and mental. Physical boundaries pertain to your personal space and physical touch, while emotional boundaries involve your feelings and personal information. Mental boundaries relate to your thoughts, values, and opinions. These boundaries maintain your integrity, protecting your sense of self and ensuring you do not lose yourself in your relationships. Healthy boundaries allow you to feel safe and respected, whereas unhealthy boundaries—either too rigid or too porous—can lead to discomfort and resentment. For instance, a healthy boundary might be setting aside time for yourself despite a busy schedule. In contrast, an unhealthy boundary might be always saying yes to others at the expense of your well-being.

Identifying your boundary needs starts with self-reflection. Reflective exercises can help you explore boundaries and understand what makes you comfortable or uncomfortable. Consider situations in the past where you felt your boundaries were violated. How did you react? What would you have preferred to happen? Recognizing these signs of boundary violations is critical to understanding your limits. Journaling can be beneficial in this process. Use prompts like, "When do I feel most respected?" or "What situations make me feel uncomfortable?" to set boundary intentions. Writing down your thoughts and feelings can clarify and guide you in establishing healthier boundaries.

To maintain your boundaries, you must communicate them to others. Use clear and assertive language to express your needs and limits. For example, instead of saying, "I do not like it when you are late," you could say, "I feel disrespected when plans are changed at the last minute. Can we agree to notify each other in advance?" This transparent communication helps others understand your boundaries without feeling attacked. Setting boundaries without guilt or fear is also essential. Remember, your boundaries are valid, and it is okay to prioritize your well-being. When you encounter pushback, stay firm and reiterate your boundaries calmly. For instance, if someone reacts negatively to your request for personal space, you might say, "I understand this is difficult, but I need this time to recharge. I appreciate your understanding."

Maintaining your boundaries consistently requires ongoing effort and reinforcement. Techniques for reinforcing boundaries include regular self-check-ins to meet your needs and adjust boundaries as necessary. To handle boundary violations calmly and assertively, you need to address the issue directly without aggression. For example, if a friend repeatedly interrupts you, you might say, "I value our conversations, but I need to finish my thoughts without interruption. Can we work on this?" Reflecting on boundary successes and challenges can also provide valuable insights. Keep a journal to document your experiences, noting what worked well and what needs improvement. This reflection helps you stay mindful of your boundaries and make necessary adjustments.

Boundary-setting is a dynamic process that evolves with your relationships and personal growth. Understanding, identifying, communicating, and maintaining your boundaries can create a foundation of respect and trust in your relationships. This practice enhances your well-being and fosters healthier, more fulfilling connections.

ADDRESSING ATTACHMENT CONFLICTS AND RESOLUTION STRATEGIES

Understanding Attachment Patterns and Triggers

Identifying attachment conflicts in relationships requires recognizing the deeper patterns beneath surface-level disagreements. These conflicts often manifest as recurring arguments over seemingly minor issues, accompanied by an underlying tension that refuses to dissipate. The most common pattern involves one partner becoming increasingly clingy as the other withdraws, creating a destructive cycle of pursuit and retreat. To understand these dynamics, partners must engage in honest self-reflection, asking questions like "What triggers my insecurity?" and "How do I react when my partner pulls away?"

These inquiries can reveal the fundamental fears and anxieties driving attachment conflicts.

Consider the illustrative case of Sarah and Tom, whose relationship struggled with attachment-related tensions. Sarah experienced intense anxiety whenever Tom didn't immediately respond to her messages, leading to frequent arguments where she accused him of insufficient care. At the same time, Tom felt overwhelmed by her constant need for reassurance. Through careful reflection, Sarah discovered that her anxiety stemmed from deep-seated abandonment fears rooted in past experiences. This crucial insight allowed the couple to address the core issue instead of treating its symptoms.

Maintaining Calm During Conflicts

The foundation of effective conflict resolution lies in maintaining composure, even when emotions run high. While challenging, this skill is essential for productive dialogue. Partners can employ deep breathing exercises, grounding practices, or simple counting methods to maintain composure. Using "I" statements proves particularly effective in expressing feelings and needs while reducing defensive reactions. For example, saying, "I feel hurt when you don't respond to my messages because it makes me feel unimportant," typically generates a more positive response than accusatory statements like "You never care about me." This approach empowers you to control your emotions and the conversation.

Creating a safe space for emotional expression requires both partners to practice validation and reassurance. Instead of dismissing or minimizing feelings, acknowledge them with statements like "I can see why you feel this way." This approach helps calm immediate emotional responses and builds a foundation of security within the relationship. Partners with anxious attachments may need extra reassurance during conflicts, making validation an essential component of the resolution process. This validation provides comfort and security, fostering a healthier relationship.

Implementing Effective Time-Out Strategies

De-escalation techniques are crucial in preventing conflicts from intensifying into significant arguments. Partners must recognize early warning signs of escalation, such as raised voices, frequent interruptions, or defensive body language. When these signs appear, implementing a structured time-out can prevent further deterioration of the conversation. However, you should never use these breaks as punishment or angry withdrawal. Instead, couples should agree on a specific duration for the time-out and set a precise time to resume the discussion.

During these intentional breaks, partners can engage in self-soothing activities and personal reflection. Deep breathing exercises, mindfulness practices, or simple grounding techniques can help restore emotional balance. The key is to use this time constructively, preparing to return to the conversation with renewed perspective and composure. Partners should also respect each other's different needs during these breaks. While some may need to process emotions alone, others might benefit from gentle reassurance about the relationship's stability.

Collaborative Problem-Solving Approaches

Shifting our views of conflicts as battles to seeing them as shared challenges can transform the resolution process. This collaborative approach emphasizes teamwork and mutual support, encouraging both partners to work together toward solutions. When discussing potential resolutions, remain open to compromise and creative solutions. For instance, Sarah and Tom developed a system where Tom would send quick acknowledgment messages when unable to fully respond while Sarah worked on managing her anxiety during these periods.

Clear communication of needs becomes fundamental in this process, particularly for those with anxious attachment styles who often harbor unexpressed expectations. Partners should engage in open discussions about their needs during and after conflicts. Understanding that one partner might need space to process while another might need immediate discussion can help establish protocols that respect both individuals' attachment styles and emotional requirements.

Post-Conflict Repair and Growth

After resolving conflicts, engaging in repair efforts helps restore emotional security and strengthen the relationship bond. These efforts might include small gestures of affection, written expressions of appreciation, or dedicated time for reconnection. Such actions demonstrate commitment to the relationship despite challenges and help rebuild emotional safety. Partners should also reflect on the conflict experience, talk about what worked well, and identify areas for improvement in their communication and resolution strategies.

Regular practice through role-playing exercises can help couples develop and refine their conflict-resolution skills. Working with hypothetical scenarios allows partners to experiment with different approaches in a low-pressure environment. For instance, partners can role-play situations where one partner feels neglected and the other feels overwhelmed, and then switch roles to understand each other's perspectives. This practice, combined with thoughtful reflection on past conflicts, builds confidence in handling future disagreements constructively.

Creating a Structured Resolution Plan

Developing a formal conflict resolution plan provides a reliable framework for addressing future disagreements. This plan should outline specific steps for approaching conflicts, including agreed-upon time-out procedures, methods for addressing triggers, and strategies for maintaining productive communication. Having such a structure helps reduce anxiety about future conflicts and provides clear guidance when emotions run high.

The plan should include regular review and adjustment periods, allowing couples to refine their approach based on experience and changing needs. This ongoing development process demonstrates a commitment to growth and mutual understanding within the relationship. Partners should also consider including preventive measures in their plan, such as regular check-ins about relationship satisfaction and scheduled times for discussing concerns before they escalate into conflicts.

While navigating attachment-related conflicts can be challenging, particularly for those with anxious attachment styles, implementing these strategies creates a foundation for healthy resolution and relationship growth. Success requires consistent effort, patience, and commitment from both partners. Through understanding attachment patterns, maintaining calm communication, using effective time-outs, engaging in collaborative problem-solving, and dedicating time to repair and reflection, couples can transform conflicts into opportunities for deepening their connection and building a more secure relationship bond.

BUILDING A SECURE ATTACHMENT WITH YOUR PARTNER

When you have a secure attachment, you enjoy a strong sense of safety and trust in your relationship. Both partners feel valued and respected. This attachment style contributes to high relationship satisfaction, fostering open communication, mutual support, and emotional intimacy. Critical behaviors of secure attachment include consistent emotional availability, genuine affection, and respect for boundaries. For example, a securely attached partner will reliably respond to emotional needs, provide comfort during distress, and offer support in pursuing personal goals. These behaviors create a stable and nurturing environment where both partners can thrive.

Behaving reliably and consistently is vital to building secure attachment in your relationship. Make a conscious effort to be dependable and predictable when interacting with your partner.

Show up when you say you will follow through on promises and be there for your partner when needed. Consistency builds trust so that you and your partner have a foundation of reliability. Emotional availability and responsiveness are also crucial. This means being present and attentive when your partner shares their feelings, ensuring you are actively listening and offering empathy and support. Did your partner have a tough day? Take the time to listen and comfort them, showing that you are emotionally attuned and responsive to their needs.

Creating rituals of connection strengthens the bond between partners. These rituals can be simple yet meaningful activities that you do regularly. An example could be setting a date night, when you spend quality time together, free from distractions. Or you could start a daily check-in routine in which you discuss your day and share your thoughts and feelings. These rituals reinforce your connection, providing consistent opportunities for bonding and intimacy. They are anchors in your relationship, reminding both partners of their commitment and lover.

Maintaining secure attachment over time requires ongoing effort and intentionality. Regular relationship check-ins are vital for assessing the health of your connection and addressing any issues that arise. Set aside time each week to discuss your relationship, discussing what is going well and what could be improved. This practice helps you stay attuned to each other's needs and prevents minor issues from escalating into more significant problems. I recommend practicing gratitude and appreciation as another powerful way to maintain a secure attachment in your relationship. Express gratitude for your partner and acknowledge their positive qualities and actions regularly. Simple gestures like saying "thank you" or writing a heartfelt note can go a long way in reinforcing your bond.

Addressing and resolving conflicts constructively is essential for maintaining secure attachment. When disputes arise, approach them with a collaborative and respectful mindset. Avoid blame and focus on finding solutions that work for both partners. Are you disagreeing about household chores? Discuss each other's perspectives and negotiate a fair plan for dividing responsibilities. This collaborative approach will help resolve the immediate issue and strengthen your partnership. That is because you are demonstrating your commitment to working together.

Finally, be sure to set continuous improvement goals so your relationship continues to grow and thrive, and identify areas where you want to strengthen your secure attachment and set actionable goals. For example, you aim to increase your emotional availability by practicing active listening or to enhance your connection by establishing new rituals. Regularly review and adjust these goals, celebrating your progress and making necessary changes. Building and maintaining secure attachment requires consistent effort, emotional availability, and intentional connection. Adopting these practices and reflecting on your attachment dynamics can create a resilient, nurturing, and deeply fulfilling relationship.

CHAPTER 7
ONGOING PERSONAL GROWTH AND DEVELOPMENT

PERSONAL GROWTH IS NOT A DESTINATION BUT A CONTINUOUS, intentional journey of self-discovery and transformation. For individuals recovering from anxious attachment, this journey represents more than a path to healing—it is a profound commitment to understanding oneself, breaking destructive patterns, and cultivating the emotional resilience necessary for healthy, secure relationships.

Recovery from anxious attachment is not about achieving a perfect state but developing a compassionate, curious approach to your inner world. Each step of growth is an act of courage—a willingness to look inward, challenge long-held beliefs, and create new, healthier ways of connecting with yourself and others. I designed this chapter as your companion and guide, offering practical strategies, insights, and tools to support your ongoing personal development.

Through self-reflection, continuous learning, professional support, and intentional lifestyle choices, you will discover that personal growth is a dynamic process of becoming. It is about learning to trust yourself, understanding your emotional landscape, and creating the conditions for lasting emotional security and meaningful relationships.

As you move through this chapter, approach each section with an open heart and a spirit of gentle curiosity. Your commitment to growth is a powerful testament to your strength, resilience, and capacity for transformation.

SELF-REFLECTION: A PATH TO EMOTIONAL AWARENESS

Self-reflection is a powerful mirror that offers a clear view of your inner world. Regularly examining your thoughts, emotions, and behaviors can enhance self-awareness and identify opportunities for personal growth. This practice is especially crucial for individuals dealing with anxiety attachment, as it empowers you to understand the roots of your emotional patterns and make conscious, intentional choices, putting you in control of your emotional well-being.

The Power of Journaling: A Tool for Self-Discovery

You will remember that I mentioned daily journaling as one of the most effective techniques for self-reflection. This transformative practice provides a safe, private space to explore your inner landscape. Through writing, you create a powerful opportunity to process complex emotions, identify behavioral patterns, gain deeper insights into your relationship anxieties, and develop greater self-understanding. It is a therapeutic tool that allows you to unpack your emotional experiences with honesty and compassion.

Different journaling approaches can support your emotional healing journey. A gratitude journal helps shift your mindset from negativity to appreciation, especially when struggling with anxiety attachment. By documenting the positive aspects of your life, you can counterbalance anxious thoughts and cultivate a more balanced emotional state.

An emotional journal is a judgment-free zone where you can freely express your anxieties, fears, and frustrations. This approach allows you to vent and explore your emotions, providing relief and ultimately alleviating stress and gaining emotional clarity. A reflective journal combines gratitude and emotional exploration to comprehensively view your daily experiences and inner responses.

Free writing emerges as a powerful technique to connect with your subconscious mind. Writing without worrying about grammar, spelling, or structure allows for a stream-of-consciousness approach that can unearth hidden thoughts and feelings. This method offers profound insights into your emotional landscape, revealing patterns and perspectives you might not discover through more structured writing.

Structured journaling prompts can guide your self-reflection, especially when dealing with anxiety attachment. Thoughtful questions can help you explore your emotional experiences more deeply. Consider exploring prompts that encourage you to examine the origins of your anxieties, recognize moments of security in your relationships, and understand your growth journey.

Implementing a Daily Self-Reflection Practice

Creating a consistent routine is essential for meaningful self-reflection. Choose a dedicated time for journaling that feels natural and sustainable. Some find morning reflections before starting the day most beneficial, while others prefer evening journaling to process daily experiences. You might combine your reflection practice with other self-care activities like walking or enjoying herbal tea, making it a holistic part of your growth routine.

Modern technology offers additional support through reflection apps and digital tools. These resources can provide journaling prompts, send helpful reminders, and offer a structured space for recording your thoughts, making the practice more accessible and consistent.

Reflection as a Decision-Making Tool

Self-reflection transcends understanding your past—it becomes a strategic approach to making intentional future choices. Before making significant decisions in your relationships, examine your core values, assess your long-term goals, and consider potential outcomes. This practice helps you align your choices with your emotional well-being, creating a more mindful approach to personal and relational challenges and instilling confidence in your decisions.

The Transformative Impact of Self-Reflection

Committing to regular self-reflection and journaling offers a path to profound personal transformation. You'll develop improved emotional intelligence, understand the roots of your anxiety attachment, and cultivate healthier relationship patterns. More importantly, you'll learn to approach yourself with greater self-compassion, making more conscious and aligned decisions.

Remember, self-reflection is a journey of continuous growth. Be patient and kind to yourself as you develop this powerful personal and emotional healing practice. Each word you write and each reflection moment brings you closer to understanding yourself more deeply and creating the relationships you desire.

RESOURCES FOR CONTINUOUS LEARNING IN ATTACHMENT RECOVERY

Learning continuously is a powerful catalyst for personal growth and emotional healing. By actively engaging your mind and cultivating curiosity, you create a dynamic pathway to understanding yourself and your relationships more deeply. Learning becomes more than an academic pursuit—it's a transformative journey of self-discovery and personal development.

Ongoing education is your gateway to becoming more adaptable, innovative, and resilient. As you expose yourself to new knowledge and perspectives, you develop the capacity to view challenges through a more nuanced lens. This approach is particularly crucial for individuals recovering from anxiety attachment. It offers tools and insights that can fundamentally reshape your approach to relationships and emotional well-being, bringing a sense of relief and hope.

Recommended Books for Attachment and Personal Growth

Amir Levine and Rachel Heller's *Attached* represents a cornerstone text for anyone navigating attachment challenges. This comprehensive book offers profound insights into how different attachment styles impact relationships, providing practical strategies for building more secure and fulfilling connections. Readers will find compassionate guidance that helps them understand their relational patterns and work toward healthier interactions.

Daniel Goleman's *Emotional Intelligence* explores how emotional awareness can transform personal and professional relationships. The book offers critical tools for understanding and managing emotions, which is especially valuable for individuals working through attachment anxiety.

Eckhart Tolle's *The Power of Now* complements these insights by emphasizing the importance of mindful presence. His teachings offer a powerful approach to reducing anxiety by anchoring oneself in the present moment. For those struggling with attachment-related stress, Tolle's work can provide a transformative perspective on managing emotional turbulence.

Online Learning: Flexible Paths to Personal Growth

Modern technology has revolutionized personal development through accessible online learning platforms. Websites like Coursera, Udemy, and Skillshare offer comprehensive courses on critical topics such as mindfulness, emotional regulation, and relationship skills. You can seamlessly integrate these courses into your daily life to provide flexible learning options.

Interactive online workshops led by personal development experts offer precious experiences. Unlike traditional learning methods, these sessions provide hands-on, practical approaches to understanding and implementing personal growth strategies. They create opportunities for direct engagement, allowing you to learn from experienced professionals while connecting with a community of people on similar journeys, fostering a sense of connection and understanding.

Embracing a Lifelong Learning Mindset

Personal growth is not a destination but a continuous journey. By consistently exposing yourself to new ideas, perspectives, and learning opportunities, you create a dynamic approach to personal development. This mindset of curiosity and openness becomes a powerful tool in your attachment recovery process.

Remember that learning takes many forms. While books and online courses are valuable, they complement other growth strategies like therapy, support groups, and personal reflection. Each resource offers a unique perspective that can contribute to your understanding and healing.

Practical Tips for Continued Learning

Consider creating a personal learning plan that includes the following:

- Regular reading time
- Scheduled online course participation
- As discussed in the previous section, journaling to reflect on new insights
- Discussing learned concepts with a therapist or support group

Your Ongoing Journey of Discovery

The approaches and resources discussed in this chapter are not mere suggestions but invitations to a deeper understanding of yourself and your relationships. Each book you read, each course you take, and each moment of reflection brings you closer to creating the secure, fulfilling connections you deserve.

Approach your learning journey with patience, compassion, and an open heart. Your commitment to personal growth is a powerful act of self-love and healing.

THE ROLE OF THERAPY AND PROFESSIONAL HELP

As we have seen, anxious attachment can significantly impact how we experience relationships. They often lead to a cycle of insecurity, a persistent need for reassurance from our partners, and a fear of abandonment. Therapy can be a transformative step for those working to overcome these challenges.

Consider seeing a therapist who specializes in inner child work. A professional can offer valuable insights and advice. Look for someone trained in trauma-informed care who makes you feel safe and supported. The right therapeutic relationship can make a significant difference, but finding a therapist who resonates with you is vital.

I worked with a therapist with over twenty years of experience in trauma-informed care. She emphasized the importance of patience and self-compassion in the healing process. Our sessions taught me that healing the inner child is like tending to a wounded part of yourself. It requires consistent care and understanding. I was given helpful exercises such as writing a dialogue between my adult self and inner child to foster communication and trust.

Here is how therapy and professional help are critical in healing and recovery.

1. **Understanding Attachment Styles**: Therapy provides a safe space for us to explore our attachment styles. A trained counselor can help us identify the roots of our anxious attachment, often tracing back to early relationships and experiences. This understanding can bring relief, allowing us to gain insight and heal, knowing that past experiences shape current behaviors and feelings.

2. **Developing Healthier Relationship Patterns**: Through therapy, we can recognize unhealthy relationship patterns,

such as clinging, excessive need for validation, or fear-driven behaviors. Therapists can guide us in developing healthier communication styles and coping strategies that promote secure attachment. This growth can lead to more stable and fulfilling relationships over time.

3. **Building Self-Esteem and Self-Worth**: Anxious attachment often stems from low self-esteem and inadequacy. Therapy can help us work on self-acceptance and self-worth, empowering them to approach relationships from a place of strength rather than neediness. As we cultivate a stronger sense of self, they become more capable of forming healthy, balanced partnerships and instilling confidence.

4. **Practicing Emotional Regulation**: Therapy offers tools and techniques for managing anxiety and emotional responses. By learning mindfulness, grounding techniques, and emotional regulation strategies, we can better handle our fears and insecurities in relationships. This practice leads to decreased anxiety and a more remarkable ability to engage in constructive interactions with partners.

5. **Creating Secure Attachments**: A therapist, with their professional training and experience, can assist us in identifying and fostering secure attachments. This may involve exploring current relationships and understanding what qualities in partners foster security versus insecurity. The therapist can guide us to seek and nurture relationships based on mutual respect and understanding, reinforcing healthier attachment styles.

6. **Establishing Boundaries**: One common struggle for those of us with anxious attachment is an inability to develop or maintain personal boundaries. Therapy encourages us to recognize and communicate our needs effectively to our partners. Establishing boundaries helps to foster respect and support within relationships, creating a more balanced dynamic.

7. **Foster Connection through Group Therapy**: Group therapy can also benefit those with anxious attachment styles. Connecting with others with similar experiences can provide validation, reduce feelings of isolation, and offer insights into different coping strategies. This communal support can reinforce healing and provide additional perspectives on forming healthy relationships, creating a sense of belonging and support.

Therapy and professional help can be invaluable resources for many of us seeking to recover from anxious attachment. Through increasing self-awareness, developing healthier relationship patterns, and learning effective coping strategies, we can break free from cycles of anxiety and insecurity. With time and commitment, therapy can pave the way for secure, loving relationships that foster personal growth and emotional fulfillment. Remember, the journey to healing and growth is unique for everyone. However, with proper support and commitment, overcoming anxious attachments and building healthier, more fulfilling relationships are possible.

LIFESTYLE CHANGES FOR LONG-TERM ANXIETY MANAGEMENT

As we have seen throughout this book, managing anxiety, particularly in the context of attachment recovery, requires thoughtful lifestyle changes that can promote emotional well-being and resilience. Here are several essential practices to consider:

1. **Develop Coping Strategies**: Learn and practice the coping mechanisms we discussed throughout the book. Having a repertoire of strategies can empower you to handle anxiety when it arises.

2. **Establish Healthy Routines**: Creating a structured daily routine can provide a sense of predictability and security. It can also be constructive for those recovering from attachment-related anxiety. For instance, wake up at the same time each day, have regular meals, and incorporate healthy activities we discussed earlier.

3. **Limit Exposure to Stressors**: Identify and minimize exposure to people, environments, or media that exacerbate anxiety. Setting boundaries in relationships and taking breaks from social media can significantly reduce overwhelming feelings.

4. **Nurture a Balanced Diet**: What we eat daily is vital to our mental health. Aim to have a balanced diet of rich, whole foods. Eat a mix of vegetables, lean protein, fruits, and whole grains. Staying adequately hydrated and reducing caffeine and sugar consumption can also contribute to lower anxiety levels.

5. **Cultivate Supportive Relationships**: Building and cultivating healthy relationships can help combat feelings of loneliness and insecurity. Foster connections with friends, family, or support groups that understand your experiences and can provide encouragement and empathy during challenging times.

6. **Seek Professional Guidance**: Consulting with a counselor or therapist specializing in attachment can provide invaluable tools and perspectives. Treatment can offer a safe space to explore underlying patterns and develop strategies for long-term recovery.

7. **Set Realistic Goals**: Establishing small and achievable goals can be a source of encouragement that can help build confidence and a sense of accomplishment. Celebrate progress, no matter how small, and be patient with yourself as you navigate the recovery process.

Making these lifestyle changes can significantly improve how you recover from anxiety related to attachment. Our recovery journeys are unique, so finding what resonates best with you and being kind to yourself throughout the process is essential.

DEVELOPING A PERSONAL GROWTH PLAN

Personal growth is a journey of change, self-discovery, and evolution—not a destination. For individuals recovering from anxious attachment, creating a structured personal growth plan becomes a beacon of hope, a crucial strategy for healing and building emotional resilience.

The Foundations of a Personal Growth Plan

A comprehensive personal growth plan goes beyond simple goal setting. It requires deep self-reflection, an honest assessment of your current emotional landscape, and a compassionate approach to personal development. The plan serves as a roadmap, helping you navigate the complex terrain of emotional healing and relationship growth.

Begin by conducting a thorough self-assessment. Examine your current emotional patterns, relationship dynamics, and most vulnerable areas. This process isn't about criticism but creating a compassionate understanding of your inner world. Consider your past relationship experiences, attachment triggers, and the emotional challenges that have consistently surfaced in your life.

Critical Components of an Effective Growth Plan

Your personal growth plan should address multiple emotional and relational well-being dimensions. Start by identifying specific areas for development. These might include:

- Emotional regulation skills
- Communication capabilities
- Self-confidence and self-trust
- Understanding and managing attachment triggers
- Developing healthier relationship patterns

Create measurable, achievable goals for each of these areas. Instead of vague intentions, craft specific objectives that you can track and celebrate. For instance, rather than saying, "I want to be less anxious," develop a goal like "I will practice three grounding techniques daily for the next three months" or "I will communicate my needs clearly in my relationship without apologizing for having them."

Implementing Your Growth Strategy

Consistency is the cornerstone of meaningful personal development. Design a daily and weekly framework that supports your growth objectives. This framework might involve the following:

- Morning meditation or journaling
- Weekly therapy or coaching sessions
- Regular self-reflection exercises
- Specific communication practice with your partner
- Dedicated time for personal learning and skill development

Technology and various resources can support your growth plan. Consider using the following:

- Habit-tracking apps
- Journaling platforms
- Online courses on emotional intelligence
- Meditation and mindfulness applications
- Support group connections

Overcoming Obstacles and Maintaining Motivation

Personal growth is not a linear path. You will encounter challenges, setbacks, and moments of doubt. Develop a resilience strategy that acknowledges these potential obstacles. Create a support system that includes professional guidance, trusted friends or family, and potentially a support group for individuals working through attachment challenges.

Embrace self-compassion throughout your journey. Understand that healing is a process, and every small step is significant. Celebrate your progress, no matter how incremental it might seem, knowing that you are caring for yourself in the best possible way.

Periodic Review and Adaptation

Your personal growth plan is a living document. Schedule regular review periods—perhaps quarterly—to assess your progress, adjust your strategies, and set new intentions. This plan might involve the following:

- Reviewing your initial goals
- Acknowledging your achievements
- Identifying new areas for development
- Adjusting your approach based on your learnings

The Holistic Nature of Personal Growth

Remember that personal growth extends beyond specific relationship skills. It encompasses your entire being—mental, emotional, physical, and spiritual. Integrate practices that nurture all these aspects, such as:

- Regular physical exercise
- Nutrition that supports mental health
- Creative expression
- Spiritual or mindfulness practices
- Continuous learning

A Journey of Transformation

Your personal growth plan is more than a series of objectives. It's a profound commitment to yourself—a declaration that you are worthy of healthy, secure relationships and inner peace. Approach this journey with patience, curiosity, and unwavering compassion for yourself.

As you move forward, trust in your capacity for change. Each step you take is toward healing, understanding, and, ultimately, the loving, secure relationships you deserve.

AFTERWORD

We have concluded our journey through the complexities of anxious attachment. You now understand the roots of this attachment style and practical strategies for overcoming it. I hope I have shown you the best path toward healthier, more secure relationships in this book.

SUMMARY OF KEY INSIGHTS

Let's reflect on what you have learned. We began by exploring the origins of anxious attachment. You learned about its evolutionary roots and the impact of early caregiving behaviors. You discovered how childhood experiences and societal influences shape your attachment style. This foundational knowledge laid the groundwork for understanding the emotional and psychological landscape you navigate daily.

We then explored the neuroscience behind attachment, examining brain structures and neurochemical processes that influence your behaviors. You gained insights into how your brain responds to stress and attachment cues and the potential for neuroplasticity to change these patterns. This knowledge has equipped you to approach your attachment style with compassion and curiosity.

It is essential to be able to identify anxious attachment in yourself. I offered tools and information you can use to achieve that, including self-assessment tools, reflective exercises, and case studies. You became more aware of your behaviors and their origins. Recognizing these patterns is the first step toward change, and your increased self-awareness paves the way for stronger, healthier relationships.

I provided practical strategies for managing anxiety, jealousy, and overthinking, including tools for immediate relief and long-term change. Self-soothing techniques, grounding exercises, cognitive-behavioral strategies, and visualization practices are now part of your toolkit. These methods empower you to regulate your emotions and reduce the intensity of your anxiety.

Enhancing self-awareness and emotional regulation through mindfulness, guided meditations, and self-compassion exercises further solidified your growth. These techniques help you stay present, manage emotions, and cultivate inner peace.

We also focused extensively on rebuilding trust and emotional security in relationships. You learned effective communication techniques, conflict resolution strategies, and ways to create a secure foundation with your partner. These are fundamental skills for fostering trust and deepening emotional intimacy.

Inner child healing was explored to address unresolved traumas and unmet needs from your past. You began a profound healing and self-compassion journey by reconnecting with your inner child. Remember the importance of this work in transforming your attachment style and building a more secure sense of self.

Another critical area was strengthening relationship skills, such as effective communication, setting boundaries, active listening, and empathetic responses. These skills are the building blocks of healthy, fulfilling relationships.

Finally, we discussed the importance of ongoing personal growth and development. You learned to continuously self-reflect, seek support from communities and resources, and create a personal growth plan. This commitment to lifelong learning ensures that your journey toward secure attachment and lasting love continues.

PRACTICE WHAT YOU LEARN AND CELEBRATE PROGRESS

As you reach the end of this book, take a moment to reflect on how far you have come. You have already taken courageous steps toward healing and growth by exploring your attachment patterns, confronting old wounds, and practicing new strategies. Your progress will be evident and should be celebrated. Remember, progress is not about perfection but about showing up for yourself each day, even when challenging. Celebrate the small victories: the moments of emotional clarity, healthier conversations, and growing trust in yourself and others. Keep practicing the tools you have learned here, knowing that every effort you make builds the foundation for a more secure and fulfilling future. You deserve love, connection, and peace—not just from your relationships but from within. Embrace this journey, stay committed to your growth, and trust that with time and persistence, you are creating a life filled with the lasting love and emotional security you have always deserved.

You now have all the fundamental knowledge and tools needed to change your attachment style and foster healthier relationships. But remember, this journey is ongoing. Actively apply the strategies and exercises this book provides to your daily life. I recommend revisiting chapters as needed and continually using the tools I provide to improve further. On a personal note, please accept my thanks for embarking on this journey with me. Your willingness to explore, reflect, and grow is inspirational. I hope I have provided valuable insights and practical tools for your journey toward healing and growth.

Remember, lasting love and secure, healthy relationships are possible. By applying the teachings of this book, you can create the fulfilling connections you deserve. Keep believing in your ability to change and grow. Your journey toward a more secure, loving future has just begun.

APPENDIX

SUPPORTING PARTNERS WITH ANXIOUS ATTACHMENT

THIS SECTION IS AIMED AT PARTNERS OF PEOPLE WITH ANXIOUS attachments. It is a short primer to give loved ones who may not understand anxious attachment and recovery and to promote open dialogue and avenues of communication and support. It also provides a different perspective for those in anxious attachment recovery of what their partners may see in the relationship.

Recognizing Anxious Attachment in Others

Recognizing anxious attachment behaviors in others is a crucial step in providing support. It requires understanding the intricate dynamics of attachment styles and recognizing the emotional needs that arise both in ourselves and those we care for. While self-awareness of our attachment patterns can often illuminate our challenges, it may be significantly different when we observe these patterns in others.

When identifying anxious attachment behaviors in someone else, we may recognize the confusion, emotional highs and lows, and the constant need for reassurance that can characterize their interactions. This awareness invites empathy as we strive to create a safe space for them to express their fears and anxieties. However, it also calls for us to remain mindful of our responses and boundaries as we navigate their emotional landscape's complexities without becoming overwhelmed.

By exploring how to support a partner or loved one through recovery, we become better equipped to foster healthier relationships while managing our emotional well-being. This journey of mutual understanding and support can lead to deeper connections, improved communication, and, ultimately, the healing of attachment wounds for both individuals involved.

Behaviors to Look Out For

Specific behavioral indicators can let you recognize signs of anxious attachment in other people. Inconsistency in how the person communicates tends to be one of the most common signs. Someone with an anxious attachment may sometimes overwhelm you with messages because they are looking for closeness and affirmation. However, another day, that person may be completely silent because they fear seeming too needy. This kind of inconsistency can be highly confusing and emotionally drains everyone involved. For example, they might often send you texts asking for reassurance that everything is okay between you, even when there has not been any evidence of issues. Their deep-seated fear of abandonment creates the person's frequent need for reassurance.

Other common signs of anxious attachment are jealousy and possessiveness. If someone has an anxious attachment, they may exhibit intense jealousy over apparently trivial interactions. They may have trouble dealing with the fact that you have relationships with other people, even if those relationships are entirely platonic. Some common manifestations of this possessiveness include constantly asking about a partner's whereabouts, who they spend time with, and what they do. They may interpret neutral behaviors as signs of disinterest or infidelity. These behaviors can create a cycle of conflict and mistrust, making fostering a healthy, balanced relationship complicated.

People with anxious attachment styles may also experience frequent emotional highs and lows, with drastic and sudden mood and behavior changes. That is why people in relationships with them sometimes feel like they are on an emotional rollercoaster. People with an anxious attachment may be affectionate and ecstatic one minute and upset and distant the next. These mood swings often result from internal conflict between their craving for closeness and fear of rejection. Partners of people with anxious attachment can find it challenging to navigate the emotional dynamics of the relationship.

How Anxious Attachment Impacts a Relationship

It is crucial to understand how much anxious attachment styles can impact the dynamics of a relationship. The frequent need for reassurance often means that there are communication problems. This can create a cycle in which the partner with anxious attachment constantly seeks validation. At the same time, a feeling of overwhelm causes the other to withdraw. This cyclical characteristic of reassurance-seeking and withdrawal can lead to less trust and a problematic pattern of conflict to get past. Both partners may have difficulty finding a stable footing because they feel constantly engaged in emotional negotiations.

These problematic relational patterns may become a fixed part of the relationship, which can cause frequent conflict. When someone with anxious attachment has intense reactions to misunderstandings and actions or words they perceive as rejection, this can cause significant conflict. With these conflict cycles, both people may end up feeling like they are walking on eggshells. Both partners will probably be hyper-aware of what the other person is feeling, wanting to avoid causing anxiety or arguments. These kinds of patterns can cause breakdowns in trust and communication, as well as feelings of being emotionally drained.

How to Support Your Partner

Empathy is vital when supporting a partner with an anxious attachment. It is essential to practice understanding and compassion in your approach to conversations about attachment. Make sure you use listening techniques, as they can be transformational when it comes to communication. If your partner wants to tell you about their anxieties and fears, listen patiently and do not interrupt. Maintain eye contact and nod, showing that you are present and attentive. Make statements like, "I know how anxious you get when I do not respond immediately." Giving them this validation of their emotions can help your partner feel heard and understood.

Make your partner feel safe in your open dialogue. This safe space will make your partner feel better about sharing their feelings without fearing being dismissed or judged. Let them know that their emotions are valid and ensure that they know you are there for them, offering support. You could ask your partner if they would like to set aside a regular time to express their feelings about the relationship and any concerns that might arise. You can significantly reduce some of your partner's anxiety by creating an environment of trust and openness.

Consistent communication and reassurance are critical strategies for supporting your partner with an anxious attachment. Check with your partner regularly and reassure them of your love and commitment. You can make your partner with anxious attachment feel much better just by sending thoughtful texts that ease their fears. Of course, you will need to set healthy boundaries while showing compassion. Communicate your limits and personal needs clearly but in a manner that is also kind and understanding. Help your partner understand that your boundaries are not a rejection and are simply necessary for you to maintain a balanced and healthy relationship.

Professional help and therapy can also benefit someone with an anxious attachment. Sometimes, a person needs more support than their partner can give. If you feel it is helpful, consider suggesting therapy as an option. Do this in a supportive way, communicating that treatment could help them develop valuable tools and coping mechanisms for anxiety management to feel secure in the relationship. Remind them that treatment can provide a safe space.

Remember, people with anxious attachments need recognition and support. If you have a partner with an anxious attachment style, you need to understand the roots of their behaviors and show empathy. This will help you build a stronger, more loving relationship.

FURTHER READING

John Bowlby's Attachment Theory, Saul McLeod, https://www.simplypsychology.org/bowlby.html

Contributions of Attachment Theory and Research: A Framework for Future Research, Translation, and Policy, Jude Cassidy et al., https://www.ncbi.nlm.nih.gov/pmc/articles/PMC4085672/

Neural basis underlying the trait of attachment anxiety and avoidance revealed by the amplitude of low-frequency fluctuations and resting-state functional connectivity, Min Deng et al., https://bmcneurosci.biomedcentral.com/articles/10.1186/s12868-021-00617-4/

Culture and Child Attachment Patterns: a Behavioral Systems Synthesis, Paul S Strand et at., https://www.ncbi.nlm.nih.gov/pmc/articles/PMC6901642/

8 Attachment Style Questionnaires & Tests to Assess Clients, Alicia Nortje, https://positivepsychology.com/attachment-style-tests/

The Power of Journaling for Well-being: A Path to Self-Discovery and Healing, https://dhwblog.dukehealth.org/the-power-of-journaling-for-well-being-a-path-to-self-discovery-and-healing/

How to Identify and Manage Your Emotional Triggers, https://www.healthline.com/health/mental-health/emotional-triggers/

Trauma of the Past: The Impact of Adverse Childhood
Experiences on Adult Attachment, Money Beliefs and Behaviors,
and Financial Transparency, Dr. Bruce Ross et al., https://newprairiepress.org/cgi/viewcontent.cgi?article=1280&context=jft/

Self-Soothing Techniques to Cope with Anxiety, Wendy Rose Gould, https://www.verywellmind.com/how-to-self-soothe-when-coping-with-anxiety-5199606/

30 Grounding Techniques to Quiet Distressing Thoughts, https://www.healthline.com/health/grounding-techniques/

An Overview of Attachment Anxiety, Arlin Cuncic, https://www.verywellmind.com/attachment-anxiety-4692761/

Eight Visualization Techniques for Stress Reduction,
https://www.betterhelp.com/advice/stress/9-visualization-techniques-for-stress-reduction/

Effective Engagement Requires Trust and Being Trustworthy, Consuelo H Wilkins, https://www.ncbi.nlm.nih.gov/pmc/articles/PMC6143205/

5 Effective Communication Techniques for Couples, https://www.counsellinginmelbourne.com.au/communication-techniques-for-couples/

Contributions of Attachment Theory and Research: A Framework for Future Research, Translation, and Policy, Jude Cassidy et al., https://www.ncbi.nlm.nih.gov/pmc/articles/PMC4085672/

Why You May Have Trust Issues and How to Overcome Them, Kendra Cherry, https://www.verywellmind.com/why-you-may-have-trust-issues-and-how-to-overcome-them-5215390/

Inner Child Healing: 35 Practical Tools for Growing Beyond Your Past, Jeremy Sutton, https://positivepsychology.com/inner-child-healing/

John Bradshaw and The Power of Inner Child Work, Joan E Childs, https://joanechilds.com/john-bradshaw-and-the-power-of-inner-child-work/

EMDR Therapy for Childhood Trauma, Shelley Flannery, https://childmind.org/article/emdr-therapy-for-childhood-trauma/

Emotion Regulation in Close Relationships: The Role of Individual Differences and Situational Context, Wan-Lan Chen et al., https://www.ncbi.nlm.nih.gov/pmc/articles/PMC8355482/

Cognitive Reappraisal, https://www.psychologytoday.com/us/basics/cognitive-reappraisal/

8 Powerful Self-Compassion Exercises & Worksheets, https://positivepsychology.com/self-compassion-exercises-worksheets/

How to Improve Your Relationships With Healthy Communication, Elizabeth Scott, https://www.verywellmind.com/managing-conflict-in-relationships-communication-tips-3144967/

Setting Healthy Boundaries in Relationships, Sheldon Reid, https://www.helpguide.org/relationships/social-connection/setting-healthy-boundaries-in-relationships/

Active Listening: A Key to Deeper Intimacy and Understanding in Your Relationship, Mara Hirschfeld, https://holdinghopemft.com/active-listening-a-key-to-deeper-intimacy-and-understanding-in-your-relationship/

What Does Secure Attachment Look and Feel Like? Plus How to Develop It, Sanjana Gupta, https://www.verywellmind.com/secure-attachment-signs-benefits-and-how-to-cultivate-it-8628802/

The Importance of Self-Reflection: How Looking Inward Can Improve Your Mental

Health, Sanjana Gupta, https://www.verywellmind.com/self-reflection-importance-benefits-and-strategies-7500858/

21 Best Emotional Intelligence Books to Improve EQ, https://positivepsychology.com/best-emotional-intelligence-books/

Support groups: Make connections, get help, https://www.mayoclinic.org/healthy-lifestyle/stress-management/in-depth/support-groups/art-20044655/